.

The Last Week

The Last Week

The seven words of Jesus from the cross on Mount Calvary

Eleazar Barajas

Library of Congress Control Number:		2022902490
ISBN:	Softcover	978-1-5065-3983-6
	eBook	978-1-5065-3984-3

Transalated by Elizabeth Barajas

Print information available on the last page.

Revision date: 02/02/2022

To order additional copies of this book, contact:
Palibrio
1663 Liberty Drive, Suite 200
Bloomington, IN 47403
Toll Free from the U.S.A 877.407.5847
Toll Free from Mexico 01.800.288.2243
Toll Free from Spain 900.866.949
From other International locations +1.812.671.9757
Fax: 01.812.355.1576
orders@palibrio.com
838242

CONTENTS

Introduction

By world tradition, the so-called Passion Week is one of the most popular of the fifty-two that make up the year. Together with Christmas, passion week, its celebrated worldwide. Although there are certain countries, some religions, some sects of Christianity and some religious groups that, for religious or political reasons, try to ignore the celebration of the Passion of Christ, the Passion of Christ Week is world famous.

Now, although I have said that the Week of the Passion of Christ is of worldwide fame, in the twenty-first century, apparently, this important week of the year, in which the decisive steps and events of the Salvific Plan are remembered, has remained in history as a mere tradition. Especially in the United States of America, this Week has ceased to be essential in church life, instead of taking the time to worship the Lord while remembering his Passion, American people use it for travel, for family parties, for sports, and the less fortunate use, for work.

In some Christian churches on Friday, they hold a one-hour service remembering the crucifixion of Jesus. On Sunday, which is Easter Sunday, some Christian churches hold a worship at 6:00 a.m., then a breakfast at 8:00 a.m., and the "celebration" of Jesus Christ's triumph over the power of sin ends in a park having fun or on the beach or at home sleeping.

In the United States of America, the passion for worship and gratitude to God during Passion Week is staying in the archives of the History of Christianity! The gospel narrative about Passion Week has been left in the old church; that is, the Contemporary Christian Church has focused on other biblical doctrines and stories. However, when we return to reading the narrative of The Last Week of Jesus' Life on This Earth, we notice that: "It's very moving. There is no interruption; one event immediately succeeds another. It's such a vivid narrative... as can be found in any other language, and from now – Palm Sunday – to the conclusion – that is, until Easter Sunday – we have before us the greatest studies to which the mind of man has ever been directed".[1]

This poignant narrative from The Last Week of Jesus' Life, the Gospels present it as follows:

"Sunday:
Jesus enters Jerusalem (Mt 21:1-11; Mk 11:1-11; Lk 19:28-44; Jn 12:12-19).
Jesus spends the night in Bethany (Mt 21:17; Mk 11:11b).

Monday:
Jesus curses a fig tree (Mt 21:18-22; Mk 11:12-14, 20-25).
Jesus goes to the Temple (Mt 21:12-16; Mk 11:15-18; Lk 19:45-48).
Jesus returns to Bethany (Mt 21:17; Mk 11:19).

---

[1]   B. H. Carroll. *Bible Commentary: The Four Gospels. Volume VI. Volume II.* Trd. Sara A. Hale. (Terrassa (Barcelona), Spain. Editorial CLIE. 1986), 262.

Tuesday:

Jesus teaches and discusses in the Temple (Mt 21:23-39; Mk 11:27-12:44; Lk 20:1-47).

The offering of the poor widow (Mt 12:41-44; Lk 21:1-4).

Jesus speaks of the destruction of the Temple and the coming of the Son of Man (Mt 24:1-25:46; Mk 13:1-37; Lk 21:5-38).

Wednesday:

The plan to kill Jesus (Mt 26:1-5; Mk 14:1-2).

Jesus in Bethany (Mt 26:6-13; Mk 14:3-9; Jn 12:1-8).

Conspiracy against Jesus (Mt 26:14-16; Mk 14:10-11; Lk 22:1-6).

Thursday:

Jesus commemorates the Passover (Mt 26:17-25; Mk 14:12-21; Lk 22:7-16).

Jesus teaches about the Lord's Supper (Mt 26:26-30; Mk 14:22-26; Lk 22:17-23; I Cor. 11:23-25).

Jesus washes the disciples' feet (Jn 13:1-20).

Jesus announces Peter's denial (Mt 26:31-35; Mk 14:27-31; Lk 22:31-34; Jn 13:36-38).

Jesus comforts the disciples (Jn 14:1-16:33).

Jesus prays on behalf of the disciples (Jn 17:1-26).

Jesus in the Garden of Gethsemane (Mt 26:36-46; Mk 14:32-42; Lk 22:39-46).

Jesus is imprisoned (Mt 26:47-56; Mk 14:43-52; Lk 22:47-52; Jn 18:1-12).

Jesus before the Council (Mt 26:57-68; Mk 14:53-65; Lk 22:54, 66-71; Jn 18:19-24).

Peter denies Jesus (Mt 26:68-75; Mk 14:66-72; Lk 22:54-62; Jn 18:15-18, 25-27).

Friday:

Jesus is condemned to death by Pilate (Mt 27:1-2, 11-31; Mk 15:1-20; Lk 23:1-25; Jn 18:28-19:16).

At nine o'clock in the morning Jesus is crucified (Mt 27:32-44; Mk 15:21-32; Lk 23:26-43; Jn 19:17-27).

At three o'clock in the afternoon Jesus dies (Mt 27:45-46; Mk 14:33-41; Lk 23:44-49; Jn 19:28-30).

A soldier wounds Jesus' side (Jn 19:31-37).

Before sunset Jesus is buried (Mt 27:57-61; Mk 14;42-47; Lk 23:50-56; Jn 19:38-42)".[2]

This book emphasizes some of the activities of Jesus and the characters that surrounded him during Thursday and Friday of this last Week in which the Passion of Christ is celebrated – or was celebrated. Although the title of this book is: The Last Week, this book does not talk about the activities of the whole week, only some of them. The emphasis of this book are the events of Thursday night and those that happened all day on Friday, emphasizing on the last seven expressions of Jesus – The Seven Words of Jesus – while he was hanging from the cross on Mount Calvary. It is thus an emphasis on the act that: "Jesus, in cooperation with his Father, came into the world expressly for

[2]   The last week of Jesus' life. *Written in the Schematic Study Bible* (Brazil. United Bible Societies. 2010), 1422

the purpose of taking up his cross and giving the most precious thing he had in ransom for all: His blood. The apostle Peter calls it " the precious blood of Christ " (I Peter 1:19)".[3]

I have set out to end this book not with a dead and buried Christ, but with a Risen and Victorious Jesus Christ over sin and death itself. In both events, the burial and resurrection of Jesus, the activities of women; the ones I have called: The Other Team of the Lord, are the protagonists of the last two events; the one that marks the end of the Last Week of Jesus Christ's life on this earth, the burial of Jesus, and the first that marks the beginning of a new age, the Resurrection of Jesus Christ.

I hope, then: First, Hispanics will read this book. Unfortunately, we are people who are interested in many things, except reading. We are people of disagreements, of strikes, people subjugated intellectually, people who love parties, but also people slow in reading. It is much easier to sit in front of the TV and watch a soap opera from beginning to end or a movie from beginning to end, this is much simpler than taking a book with our hands, like this one, and reading it. I hope I am wrong with some of you who have already started reading these pages.

Second, I hope that reading this book will motivate us that The Week of the Passion of Christ does not remain in the archives of ecclesiastical history, but that it will again be a practice of worship in our Christian churches.

In Christ:

Eleazar Barajas
La Habra, California.

---

[3] Santiago Wadel. God is... Some attributes of God. The good God. (Costa Rica, C. A. Publicadora la Merced. 2021. Article published in the magazine La Antorcha de la Verdad. March-April 2021. Volume 35. Number 2.), 9.

PROPHETIC FULFILLMENT

"When they were already near Jerusalem and had reached Bethphage, the Mount of Olives, Jesus sent two of his disciples, telling them, 'Go to the village that is in front. There they will find a female donkey tied up, and a male donkey with her. Untie her and bring them to me. ... This happened so that what the prophet said, would be fulfilled:

'Say to the city of Zion: 'Look, your King comes to you, humble, riding on a donkey, on a donkey, raising a beast of burden'.

There were a lot of people. Some laid their cloaks along the way, and others laid branches that were cut from the trees. And both of those who were in front and those who were behind, shouted, 'Hosana to the Son of King David! Blessed is he who comes in the name of the Lord! Hosana in the heights!

When Jesus entered Jerusalem, the whole city was in a rampage, and many asked, "Who is this?' And the people answered, 'It is the prophet Jesus, the prophet of Nazareth of Galilee'."

Matthew 21:1-11, (DHH).

INTRODUCTION.

We begin this series of preaching with the activity of Jesus on the first day of the week called: Week of the Passion of Christ. That is, we begin with Jesus' entry into the city of Jerusalem with surprising joy. The people of Jerusalem were glad to see Jesus' riding on a donkey entering their city.

Are you not surprised by this reaction of the people of Jerusalem? Especially in the last two years of Jesus' life, the Lord had made Himself hated by the religious leaders of His country; Jesus was teaching a new doctrine, he was correctly interpreting the Old Testament, and this practice was not accepted by the religious leadership of his day, so they hated him. But, on that first day of The Last Week of Jesus' Life, the people welcomed him to their capital city. All this was within the prophetic fulfillment.

The Christian Church took this act from Jesus and named it "Palm Sunday" and put it into practice to this day. "Palm Sunday is a religious celebration in which most of the confessions of Christianity commemorate the entry of Jesus Christ into Jerusalem, beginning Holy Week. It is a movable Christian holiday that falls on the Sunday before Easter, that is, the sixth Sunday of Lent.

The feast commemorates Jesus' Triumphal Entry into the city of Jerusalem, an event mentioned in each of the four canonical gospels. Palm Sunday marks the first day of Holy Week".[4]

---

[4]   Wikipedia, the free encyclopedia. *Palm Sunday*. (La Habra, California. Internet. Retrieved May 13, 2021), ¿https://es.wikipedia.org/wiki/Domingo de Ramos

Palm Sunday! "This is the first time Sunday has become prominent as the first day of the week. -Notice that - On the first day of the week, Christ is proclaimed King; on the first day of the week Jesus rises from the dead; on the first day of the week, Jesus appears after he has risen from the dead; on the first day of the week, he pours out the Holy Spirit upon his church. From that time onwards Sunday will be prominent".[5]

The Triumphal Entry of Jesus into the city of Jerusalem, on that Palm Sunday, was an event of a threefold prophetic fulfillment. So, we ask ourselves: Why is this event regarded as the fulfillment of prophecies? It is considered so because it refers to at least three prophetic events that were fulfilled on that first day of the Last Week of Jesus' life.

I.- JESUS WAS RECEIVED AS KING.

This is the first of the Old Testament prophecies that Jesus Christ fulfilled that first day of the week, of The Last Week of Earthly Life of the Savior of the world. The Evangelist Matthew says, "Say to the city of Zion, 'Look, your King comes to you, humble, riding on a donkey, on a donkey, raising a beast of burden'."[6] Jesus left Galilee and crossed the territory of Perea and Judea. When he was near Jerusalem, that is, when he had: "come to Bethphage (today it is called *el-Azariyeth*), to the Mount of Olives, Jesus sent two of his disciples to get him a small donkey. He rode on it and thus entered the great capital of Israel".[7] We don't know what

---

[5]   B. H. Carroll. *Bible Commentary: The Four Gospels. Volume VI. Volume II.* Trd. Sara A. Hale. (Terrassa (Barcelona), Spain. Editorial CLIE. 1986), 263.

[6]   Matthew 21:5, (DHH).

[7]   Michael J. Wilkins, *Comentario Bíblico con Aplicación: MATEO: Del texto bíblico a una Aplicación Contemporánea.* (Nashville, Tennessee, USA. Editorial Vida. 2016), 685

exactly the disciples understood when Jesus gave him the order to go and untie the donkey and her calf, Matthew says Jesus told them, "If someone says something to you, tell him, 'The Lord needs you".[8] The term Lord in Greek is Kyrios. A word that can be translated as the Master or the owner. "It can designate the earthly master or the deity in which it is believed. It is used in allusion to the master of the slave in Matthew 10:24, but also to God as the Lord of the harvest (Mt 9:38), the Lord of the vineyard (Mt 20:8), the Lord of heaven and earth and often Jesus as the Messiah (Acts 10:36)".[9]

Whether or not the disciples and people understood that Jesus was God's Kyrios, we don't know. The truth is that people received it with honors; the same honors that were done to a king who returned victorious from the war. The Evangelist Matthew says that: "There were many people. Some laid their cloaks along the way, and others tended branches that they cut from the trees".[10] "This was a festive way of receiving kings and other high authorities (2 Kings 9:13)".[11] This was a welcome as Matthew's account says with many people. At that time of the Passover: "*There were many people*" in the city of Jerusalem. The King James Version says that: "The crowd, which was very numerous, stretched out their cloaks along the way; ...".[12]

Let us remember that: "It was the time of the Passover, and Jerusalem and the whole country around it was crowded with pilgrims. Thirty years after Jesus' Triumphal Entry into Jerusalem, a governor had to take a census of the lambs that

---

[8]   Matthew 21:3, (KJ, 60).

[9]   Michael J. Wilkins, *Bible Commentary with Application: MATTHEW: From the Biblical Text to a Contemporary Application*. (Nashville, Tennessee, USA. Editorial Vida. 2016), 685

[10]   21:8, (DHH).

[11]   Footnote in the *Schematic Study Bible* (Brazil. United Bible Societies. 2010), 1423

[12]   Matthew 21:8, (KJ, 1960).

were killed in Jerusalem for the Passover and found that their number was approaching one million. The rule of the Passover was that at least ten people had to gather for each lamb, which means that on that Passover there were more than two and a half million people in Jerusalem".[13] With good reason, Matthew says that *"there were many people."*

So, if we follow the context of the account of Jesus' Triumphant Entry into the city of Jerusalem, on that first day of The Last Week, the people of Jerusalem welcomed the King of kings and Lord of lords.[14] This reception, unexpected but prophetic, was precisely "so that what was said by the prophet Zechariah may be fulfilled".[15] The prophecy says, "Rejoice much, daughter of Zion! Cry out with joy, daughter of Jerusalem! Look, your king comes to you, righteous, Savior and humble. It comes mounted on a donkey, on a colt, donkey breeding".[16] And, Jesus entered the city of Jerusalem riding on a donkey! Jesus fulfilled the prophecy spoken by Zechariah!

It should be noted that: "Those who accept Christ as King and Lord of their lives, have to place everything under his feet".[17] Dr. Michael J. Wilkins says, "The crescendo movement of Jesus' ministry appears when he enters Jerusalem, the city of the great king (Ps 48:1-2), the center of Israel's spiritual life and messianic hope".[18] Jesus entered the city of the great king

---

[13]   William Barclay. *Commentary on the New Testament: Volume 2: MATTHEW: II.* Trd. Alberto Araujo. (Terrassa (Barcelona), Spain. Editorial CLIE. 1997), 277-278
[14]   Revelation 17:14; 19:16, (KJ, 1960).
[15]   Matthew 21:4, (NIV).
[16]   Zechariah 9:9, (NIV).
[17]   Matthew Henry. *Exegetical-Devotional Commentary on the Entire Bible: Matthew.* Td. Francisco Lacueva. (Terrassa (Barcelona), Spain. Editorial CLIE. 1984), 397.
[18]   Michael J. Wilkins, *Bible Commentary with Application: MATTHEW: From the Biblical Text to a Contemporary Application.* (Nashville, Tennessee, USA. Editorial Vida. 2016), 683

and was received as a Great King! So: "The event was a living fulfillment of the Scriptures and identified the Messiah".[19]

One of Jesus' characteristics was that he traveled a lot. All the journeys narrated by the evangelists Matthew, Mark, Luke, and John, he made them walk. However: "Only once in his life did Jesus' travel in triumph, and it was precisely when he entered Jerusalem to suffer and die".[20] In that prophetic fulfillment, "Jesus could not have chosen a more dramatic moment. He went to a city crowded with people and full of religious expectations".[21] Jesus Christ came to faithfully fulfill all the prophecies and this one of the prophet Zechariah, fulfilled it perfectly. Only God can do such a thing.

II.- PROPHETIC FULFILLMENT OF THE PROPHECY OF DANIEL 9:25.

Part of Daniel's prophecy regarding Jewish messianism says that: "For one more week, he will make a covenant with many people, but in the middle of the week he will put an end to the sacrifices and offerings. And a horrible sacrilege will be committed before the altar of sacrifices, until the determined destruction falls on the author of these horrors".[22] The prophet Daniel, while in Babylonian captivity, one day began to pray for the people of Israel. "In this prayer, Daniel confesses to God his own sins and those of his people (Dan 9:4, 20). He is concerned with the prophecy spoken by the

---

[19]   B. H. Carroll. *Bible Commentary: The Four Gospels. Volume VI. Volume II.* Trd. Sara A. Hale. (Terrassa (Barcelona), Spain. Editorial CLIE. 1986), 264.

[20]   Matthew Henry. *Exegetical-Devotional Commentary on the Entire Bible: Matthew.* Td. Francisco Lacueva. (Terrassa (Barcelona), Spain. Editorial CLIE. 1984), 395.

[21]   William Barclay. *Commentary on the New Testament: Volume 2: MATTHEW: II.* Trd. Alberto Araujo. (Terrassa (Barcelona), Spain. Editorial CLIE. 1997), 278.

[22]   Daniel 9:27, (DHH).

prophet Jeremiah concerning the seventy years, during which the city of Jerusalem was razed to the ground, and asked God to restore the temple (v.17, 20)".[23]

Still, Daniel, was praying when God's answer came to him.[24] Part of that divine answer says: "He knows, then, and understands, that, from the departure of the order to restore and build Jerusalem to the Messiah Prince, there will be seven weeks, and sixty-two weeks; the square and the wall will be rebuilt in distressing times. And after sixty-two weeks the Messiah will be taken his life".[25] Another version says, "Now listen and understand! Seven sets of seven plus sixty-two sets of seven will pass from the time the order to rebuild Jerusalem is given until a ruler, the Anointed One, comes. Jerusalem will be rebuilt with streets and strong defenses, despite the perilous times".[26]

In Daniel 9:24, it says, "Seventy weeks have been decreed for your people and your holy city to put an end to their transgressions and sins, ask forgiveness for their wickedness, establish righteousness forever, seal the vision and prophecy, and sanctify the most holy place". "The word 'weeks' mentioned in this verse is in Hebrew 'shavuim' and in Greek it is 'hebdomades'. It literally means 'seven'."[27] On the term Weeks, "almost all scholars agree that this term represents 490 years".[28] However, on these texts "three perspectives are held:

---

[23] Commentary on *the Schematic Study Bible*. (Brazil. United Bible Societies. 2010), 1280.

[24] Daniel 9:20-27

[25] Daniel 9:25-26, (KJ, 1960).

[26] Daniel 9:25, (NTV).

[27] Kittim Silva Bermudes. *Daniel: History and Prophecy*. (Viladecavalls, (Barcelona), Spain. Editorial CLIE. 2014), 169-170

[28] Commentary on *the NIV Bible of Archaeological Study: An Illustrated Journey to Raves of Biblical Culture and History*. (Miami, Florida. Editorial Vida. 2009), 1440-1441.

1. The critical view postulates that the 'prophecy' was written by a pseudo-Daniel in 165 B.C.

2. The Dispensation Perspective considers that the sixty-ninth week ends before the crucifixion of Jesus and leaves the seventy weeks (the present era as a 'great parenthesis') to be fulfilled in the great tribulation".[29] However, we must note that: "These seventy sevens or weeks have nothing to do with the church. Nor have they been appointed to the Gentile nations. The angel – Gabriel – said to Daniel: 'Seventy weeks are determined upon your people and upon your holy city'. Daniel's people were the Jews, and the holy city was Jerusalem".[30]

3. The conservative or traditional view asserts that the seventy week was introduced by Jesus' baptism divided into two (three and a half years) by his death, thus causing the sacrifices to cease (Dan. 9:27)".[31]

We are left with the third. Why? Because we believe that: "Palm Sunday was the fulfillment of the prophecy of the 'seventy sevens' of the prophet Daniel: - who says – 'Know, then, and understand, that, from the departure of the order to restore and build Jerusalem to the Messiah Prince, there will be seven weeks, and sixty-two weeks; the square and the wall will be rebuilt in distressing times'. (Daniel 9:25). - Then -, John 1:11 tells us: '[Jesus] came to his own, and his own did not receive him'. The same crowds shouting, 'Hosanna!'

[29]   Commentary on *the NIV Bible of Archaeological Study: An Illustrated Journey to Raves of Biblical Culture and History.* (Miami, Florida. Editorial Vida. 2009), 1440-1441.

[30]   Kittim Silva Bermudes. Daniel: History and Prophecy. (Viladecavalls, (Barcelona), Spain. Editorial CLIE. 2014), 169-170-171

[31]   Commentary on *the NIV Bible of Archaeological Study: An Illustrated Journey to Raves of Biblical Culture and History.* (Miami, Florida. Editorial Vida. 2009), 1441.

shouted 'Be crucified!' five days later (Matthew 27:22-23)".[32]
This is, Jesus faithfully fulfilled the prophecy of Daniel 9:25.

To close this prophetic fulfillment on Jesus' part, let
us note that: "In a culminating week, Jesus concludes the
primary purpose of His Earthly Mission: The Redemption
of Humanity".[33] A prophetic plan that, again, was fulfilled
to the letter in the order and theological prophetic tradition,
for Matthew's account says that Jesus, "riding on a donkey,
on a donkey, raising a beast of burden",[34] entered the city of
Jerusalem.

From the point of view of Biblical Theology, it is noted
that Jesus fulfilled Daniel's prophecy, because, when he
entered riding on a donkey, the fact manifests that Jesus rode
on an animal in which no one had ever ridden before. It was
all a well-defined purpose: Faithfully fulfilling the Scriptures!

The Bible says that: "The red calf that was used for
purification ceremonies was to be an animal 'upon which no
yoke had been placed' (Numbers 19:2; Deuteronomy 21:3);
the wagon in which the Ark of the Lord was carried was to
be one that had not before been used for any other purpose (I
Samuel 3:7). The special sanctity of the occasion – of Palm
Sunday – was underlined by the fact that no person had
ridden on the donkey – or a calf – before".[35] Nothing adrift or
imagination! All prophecy was faithfully fulfilled! Only God
can do such a thing, so and much more, Jesus Christ IS God!

---

[32] GotQuestions.org > Spanish. *What is Palm Sunday?* (La Habra, California. Internet.
      Retrieved May 13, 2021), ¿? https://www.gotquestions.org/Espanol/Domingo-de-
      Ramos.html

[33] Michael J. Wilkins, *Bible Commentary with Application: MATTHEW: From the
      Biblical Text to a Contemporary Application.* (Nashville, Tennessee, USA. Editorial
      Vida. 2016), 684

[34] Matthew 21:5, (DHH).

[35] William Barclay. *Commentary on the New Testament: Volume 2: MATTHEW: II.*
      Trd. Alberto Araujo. (Terrassa (Barcelona), Spain. Editorial CLIE. 1997), 278.

III.- PROPHETIC FULFILLMENT OF THE PURPOSE OF THE MOSAIC LAW.

The Pauline teaching regarding one of the purposes of the law was that: "Before this faith came, the law had us imprisoned, locked up until the faith was revealed. So, the law became our guide in leading us to Christ, so that we might be justified by faith. But now that faith has come, we are no longer subject to the guide".[36] apostle Paul told the brothers of Galatia that: "Before the way of faith in Christ was opened to us, we were watched over by the law. He kept us in protective custody, so to speak, until the way of faith was revealed. Put another way, the law was our guardian until Christ came; He protected us until we were declared righteous before God through faith".[37] This is the Pauline teaching. The apostle Paul continues his teaching and says, "But now that faith has come, we are no longer in charge of that slave who was the law, for by faith in Christ Jesus you are all children of God, for, by joining Christ in baptism, you have been clothed with Christ".[38]

So, the Law of Moses was given as a guardian – *someone like the slave who watches over the children, until Christ came*, the Law of Moses was a conductive institution to lead Israel toward Christ. For the apostle Paul, the Mosaic Law was like the paidagogos among Greek culture, this was a slave, he was not the teacher, although he took much of the teaching and education of the child. The slave or paidagogos: "He was in charge of the moral welfare of the child, and it was his duty to check that he acquired the essential qualities of true manhood".[39]

---

[36] Galatians 3:23-25, (NIV).
[37] Galatians 3:23-24, (NTV).
[38] Galatians 3:23-27, (DHH).
[39] William Barclay. *Commentary on the New Testament: Volume 10: Galatians and Ephesians*. (Terrassa (Barcelona), Spain. Editorial CLIE. 1970), 53

In a good biblical hermeneutic we note that: "The Law of Moses was highly symbolic and full of similarities, which pointed to Christ and his future Atonement".[40] But, never was the law of Moses a means of salvation, but it was a conduit to become saved, that is, the law led the person to look to the Savior whom they considered as the Messiah of God. In the New Testament, this Messiah of God is Christ Jesus. He is the Master! It is, therefore, Jesus Christ, the only means of salvation.

Let us remember that in his preface to the Ten Commandments God said, "I am the Lord your God. I took you out of Egypt, out of the country where you were a slave. Don't have any other gods besides me".[41] In saying this, the Lord Almighty reminded Israel that the purpose of the law was to make them free and thus preserve them. It was a prophetic reminder that "when the set time was fulfilled, God sent his Son, born of a woman and subject to the law. God sent him to buy the freedom of those of us who were slaves of the law".[42] So it was that the prophetic fulfillment of the purpose of the Mosaic Law was fulfilled to the letter and, that day called Palm Sunday testifies to it as true.

If with the fulfillment of the law a person was not saved, then why did God give the law to the Israelites? "The Bible gives at least four reasons why God gave the Mosaic Law to His people: for His own sake, to reveal Himself to them, to differentiate them in order to reveal Himself to others, and to reveal mankind's need for a savior".[43]

[40]   Church of Jesus Christ of Latter-day Saints. *The Mosaic Law: A Preparatory Gospel: Exodus 21-24; 31-35*. (La Habra, California. Internet. Article retrieved May 14, 2021), ¿? https://www.churchofjesuschrist.org/study/manual/old-testament-student-manual-genesis-2-samuel/exodus-21-24-31-35?lang=spa

[41]   Exodus 20:2-3, (NIV).

[42]   Galatians 4:4-5, (NTV).

[43]   Compelling Truth. *Why did God give the Mosaic Law?* (La Habra, California. Internet. Article retrieved May 14, 2021), ¿? https://www.compellingtruth.org/Espanol/ley-mosaica.html

"In his letter to the Galatians, Paul explains, 'So the law became our guide in leading us to Christ, that we might be justified by faith'. (Galatians 3:24). Our need for God's saving grace through Jesus is only clear to us if we have an established standard like the Mosaic Law".[44] So, with Jesus' Triumphal Entry into the city of Jerusalem on that Palm Sunday, he announced that prophecy regarding the fulfillment of the Mosaic law had arrived! The Savior who pointed to the law, entered the city as the Sovereign that he was. Palm Sunday certified that Jesus was God's Messiah!

CONCLUSION.

God, through the prophet Isaiah, some seven hundred years before Jesus walked the streets, avenues, valleys, and mountains of Palestine, preaching the Lord's message, said, "... the word that comes out of my mouth: It will not return to me empty, but will do what I desire and fulfill my purposes".[45]

The Last Week of Jesus' life on this earth begins with the assertion that God's word fulfills his purposes. We have noticed that three of the great prophecies were fulfilled in the ministry of Christ Jesus in that Last Week.

So, Jesus Christ is King of kings, in Jesus Christ the prophecies said by Daniel were fulfilled and in the Lord Jesus himself the prophetic Fulfillment of the purpose of the Mosaic Law was realized. What do I want to tell you today? Two things:

---

[44] Compelling Truth. *Why did God give the Mosaic Law?* (La Habra, California. Internet. Article retrieved May 14, 2021), ¿? https://www.compellingtruth.org/ Espanol/ley-mosaica.html

[45] Isaiah 55:11, (NIV).

First: That you can trust what the Bible says, even if some of its prophecies go a long time without being fulfilled; The Bible is Truthful, It is the Word of God!

Second: That Jesus of Nazareth fulfilled everything one hundred percent of what was written of him. So, Jesus Christ can be trusted because he, even in the Last Week of his life, was and is the Faithful Savior King. The people of Jerusalem announced him like this and begged him for salvation. The term "Hosana" that people shouted as Jesus entered the city of Jerusalem, means "Save now."

So, Jesus, upon entering the city of Jerusalem on that first Sunday highlighted in Scripture and known as Palm Sunday, not only presented himself as the prophet of God fulfilling the Old Testament prophecies, but also did so as the promised Savior. Jesus Christ is King and Savior of the World!

Amen!

THE LAST SUPPER

"On the first day of the feast when unleavened bread was eaten, the disciples came to Jesus and asked, 'Where do you want us to prepare the Passover meal for you? He answered them, "Go to the city, to Doe's house, and say to him, 'The Master says, My hour is near, and I am going to your house to celebrate Easter with my disciples.' The disciples did as Jesus had commanded them, and they prepared the Passover meal".
Matthew 26:17-19, (DHH).

INTRODUCTION.

Like a Jew who was Jesus of Nazareth, he went to the feast called the Passover. It is also called the Feast of Unleavened Bread. This was "a feast that lasted a week and was commemorated from the 15th to the 21st of the month of Nisan – this month corresponds in our calendar to the days end of March and the beginning of April – Along with this feast, on the first day Easter was celebrated".[46]

Among all the Jewish holidays, Passover was one of the most important. So, we must ask ourselves; What was Passover and what did it mean? In a very summary, we say that: "For the Jewish religion, Passover (also known as *Pesaj* by its Hebrew name) is a solemn holiday that celebrates the freedom of the Hebrew people from the slavery of Egypt, recounted in the book of Exodus, in the Old Testament of the Bible".[47]

Based on this feast and Jesus Christ's participation in this last Jewish feast during his earthly life, we must ask ourselves some questions, three of which are:

I.- WHERE DO YOU WANT US TO PREPARE YOUR EASTER DINNER?

This is the question that the disciples asked Jesus. They knew that Their Master, as a good Jew that he was, would celebrate this important feast, and so they asked Him this question: Where do you want us to prepare the Passover meal for you? They were willing to serve Their Lord in all that He needed.

To reinforce the history of Passover practice, let us remember that: "Passover began with the ritual supper, shortly after sunset that began on the fifteenth day of the month of Nisan (the Jews counted the days from sunset). The main food at the Passover meal was the lamb; he was to have been sacrificed in the Temple according to the law, on the evening

---

[46]   Footnote commentary on *the Schematic Study Bible*. (Brazil. United Bible Societies. 2010), 1434.

[47]   Religion and spirituality. *Meaning of Jewish Passover*. What is Passover Jewish. (La Habra, California. Internet. Retrieved June 29, 2021), ¿? https://www.significados. com/pascua-judia/

of the fourteenth day, so it is likely that all the pilgrims would try to arrive a day or two before to prepare".[48] This means that Jesus, since the Tuesday of The Last Week of his earthly life, was already on the edge of the city of Jerusalem. According to the Gospel of Matthew, Jesus was in Bethany.[49] It was a village very close to Jerusalem: "Bethany was a village on the slope of the Mount of Olives, about 3.2 kilometers from Jerusalem. It was the home of Mary, Martha, and Lazarus".[50]

It is interesting to note that despite all the political, social, and religious problems that the people of Israel had gone through, Jerusalem remained the beloved city. They came to her from all over to celebrate Easter, it was a time of joyful and solemn celebration at the same time. At the end of the Easter feast, part of Psalm 128 was recited to bid farewell to the pilgrims. It was a blessing that everyone expected to hear before returning home. A blessing that says, "May the Lord bless you from Mount Zion! May you see the well-being of Jerusalem every day of your life! May you get to see your grandchildren! May there be peace in Israel!"[51]

For Jesus Christ, the city of Jerusalem was also highly appreciated, and in The Last Week of His earthly life He came to it to lay down his life for its inhabitants. Let us remember the lament of Jesus who, months before *The Last Week* of his earthly life, made in relation to the beloved city. He had said: "Jerusalem, Jerusalem, that you kill the prophets and stone the messengers that God sends you! How many times did I want to gather your children, like the hen gathers her chicks

---

[48]   Gonzalo Ang. (director). Reader's Digest. *Jesus and His Time*. The Easter pilgrimage. (México. Rider's Digest México S.A. de C.V. 2000), 120.

[49]   Matthew 26:6.

[50]   Footnote *Commentary on the NVI Bible of Archaeological Study: An Illustrated Journey to Raves of Biblical Culture and History*. (Miami, Florida. Editorial Vida. 2009), 1640.

[51]   Psalm 128:5-6, (DHH).

under the wings, but you didn't want to!"[52] It was the beloved city! And it is about this city that Jesus had expressed "his great longing to care for and protect Jerusalem as the hen cares for her chicks... Is there an image more tender than this? However, the chicks did not want to stay in the nest".[53]

So, when the disciples asked him, "Where do you want us to prepare the Passover meal for you? He answered them, go to the city, to so and so's house, and say to him, 'The Master says, My hour is near, and I am going to your house to celebrate Easter with my disciples'." (Mt 26:18). The feast of the Passover in The Last Week of the Life of Jesus Christ needed the Lamb of God who would give them true freedom, not politics, for this is temporary, but freedom from sins. This freedom that Jesus Christ offered during his ministry and that he confirmed on the Passover Feast in Jerusalem, was a liberation to have eternal life even though *the chicks* – that is, the inhabitants of Jerusalem – did not appreciate the Lamb of God.

Now, my dear brother, my dear sister in Christ and you my friend, you no longer must prepare a place to celebrate the Passover with Jesus Christ, what you must prepare is your heart or your life to receive Jesus Christ in your heart. If you do this, then you will have a true Passover Supper with Jesus Christ! you will have a true fellowship with Jesus Christ!

II.- WHAT DO THE WORDS OF JESUS MEAN WHEN HE SAID: "MY TIME IS NEAR"?

Against the background of liberation, the seven days that this festival lasted, the people rejoiced thinking about their

---

[52]   Luke 13:34, (DHH).

[53]   Darrell L. Bock. *Bible Commentary with Application: LUCAS. From the biblical text to a contemporary application.* (Miami, Florida. Editorial Vida. 2011), 349.

early liberation from Roman power. During the seven days of the festival, the longing for liberation was perceived in the air of the city of Jerusalem. And, at this last Passover supper of Jesus during his earthly ministry, the longing for deliverance, now from sin, was a few hours away from being a reality: The Messiah who would deliver you was in Jerusalem!

So, when Jesus said that his time was near, I believe that Jesus, in his sovereign omniscience knew perfectly well that his time of earthly ministry present in human form had come to an end, and it was, The Last Week of His life on this earth as a human being! This is, we talk about its omniscience. And when we touch on this subject, then, we must recognize that only God can know the exact times and events; I am saying that if Jesus knew that his time of earthly life had come, it is because, He is God!

We do not doubt at all that Jesus was a person of flesh and blood like any other human being, but, in addition, he was and IS a divine being who, unlike human beings, knows very well the times and events not so the human being who, his knowledge is very limited, does not yet know how the day in which he is living will end. The Preacher, speaking of the knowledge of the human being, said: "On the other hand, no one ever knows when his time will come just as the fish are caught in the net and the birds in the trap, so also man, when he least expects it, is caught in a bad moment".[54]

Well, the disciples had asked him where he would like to celebrate the Passover Meal. When Jesus answered their question, then, "The disciples did as Jesus had commanded them, and they prepared the Passover meal".[55] When everything was ready, according to custom, Jesus sat by the table with the

---

[54] Ecclesiastes 9:12, (DHH
[55] Matthew 26:19, (DHH).

Twelve, there was also Judas, Jesus did not set him aside, did not shame him, did not scold him for the misuse of offerings, did not reveal the intentions of Judas who, without a doubt, Jesus knew them, that is why he told them that one of them was going to deliver him and, nor did he run from the companionship of that last Easter night. Jesus Christ does not discriminate against anyone! All human beings are of utmost importance to him. Jesus died for every race of the world "that whosoever believes in him may not be lost but may have eternal life." That is, the Lamb of God who was about to be crucified, guaranteed a salvation or spiritual liberation for all those who, by faith, received him in their hearts as their personal Lord and Savior.

"According to the law, they were to take one lamb per family; Christ's disciples were his family",[56] and Judas was part of it. Jesus never made a difference among His Family! There was very close in Jesus' heart a sword that was ready to pierce him, and yet his family was of the utmost importance. No matter who you are and what you think of Jesus Christ, he has done and will continue to do whatever it takes to support you or attract you to his family.

III.- WHAT ARE THE DIFFERENCES BETWEEN THE PASSOVER OF EGYPT AND THAT OF JERUSALEM?

From the biblical account of the Exodus and also from the history of the people of Israel, we know that: "The Passover celebrated the liberation of the Jewish people from their ancestral slavery, and *Pesaj*, the name of the feast was derived

---

[56]   Matthew Henry. *Exegetical-Devotional Commentary on the Entire Bible: Matthew.* Td. Francisco Lacueva. (Terrassa (Barcelona), Spain. Editorial CLIE. 1984), 503.

from the promise of God",[57] made in Exodus 12:12-14, which says, "That night I will pass through all the city of Egypt, and I will hurt to death the eldest son of every Egyptian family and the first offspring of their animals, and I will pass sentence against all the gods of Egypt. I, the Lord, have said so. The blood will help you to point out the houses where you are. And so, when I wound the Egyptians to death, none of you will die, for I will see the blood and pass by. This is a day that you should remember and celebrate with a great feast in honor of the Lord. They will celebrate it as a permanent law that will pass from parents to children".[58]

With this historical and literary background, we note at least four differences between the Passover in Egypt and the one celebrated by Jesus Christ in the city of Jerusalem. These four differences are:

A.- *The death of human and animal firstborns.* That Easter night in Egypt, he had a divine sentence that said, "... I will hurt to death the eldest son of every Egyptian family and the first offspring of their animals".[59] That Easter night in Egypt, the sentence was served. The Bible says that; "At midnight the Lord mortally wounded the eldest son of every Egyptian family, as well as the eldest son of the pharaoh who occupied the throne, as well as the eldest son of the one who was imprisoned in prison, and also the first offspring of the animals".[60]

In the celebration of the Passover Feast in Jerusalem, only one died, Jesus Christ was the only Lamb of God who gave

---

[57] Gonzalo Ang. (director). Reader's Digest. *Jesus and His Time*. The Easter pilgrimage. (Mexico. Rider's Digest México S.A. de C.V. 2000), 121.

[58] 12:12-14, (DHH).

[59] Exodus 12:12.

[60] Exodus 12:29 (DHH).

his life. He delivered it so he could rescue humanity. On the Passover Feast celebrated by Jesus Christ in Jerusalem; Only the begotten and at the same time the firstborn of the Lord Almighty died!

B.- *Prophetic fulfillment.* Years ago, when Jesus was presented in the Temple of Jerusalem, two characters were presented who, with their prophetic spirit, announced part of the events of *The Last Week* of Jesus' life on this earth. The account that Dr. Lucas makes about what happened on that day says: "At that time there lived in Jerusalem a man named Simeon. He was a righteous and pious man, who awaited the restoration of Israel. The Holy Spirit was with Simeon and had let him know that he would not die without first seeing the Messiah, whom the Lord would send. Led by the Holy Spirit, Simeon went to the temple; and when the parents of the child Jesus also took him, to fulfill what the law commanded, Simeon took him in his arms and praised God, saying:

'Now, Lord, your promise is fulfilled: you can let your servant die in peace. For I have already seen the salvation which you have begun to accomplish in the sight of all peoples, the light which will illuminate the nations, and which will be the glory of your people Israel'. Simeon who was then high priest the father and mother of Jesus were amazed to hear what Simeon said of the child.

Then Simeon gave them his blessing, and he said to Mary, the mother of Jesus, "Look, this child is destined to cause many in Israel to fall or rise. He will be a sign that many will reject, so that the intentions of many hearts will be laid bare. But all this is going to be for you like a sword that goes through your own soul".[61]

---

[61]   Luke 2:33-35, (DHH).

Simeon referred to the rejection that Jesus would suffer in his Earthly Ministry and that he would take him to the cross of the Calvary, an act that, for his mother Mary, would be as painful as a sword that would be piercing her own soul. When the holy writer speaks of a sword that pierced Mary's soul, then he refers to the therefore: "This will be the result of Israel's rejection of the Messiah (Jn 18:25)".[62] This was also the same sword that Jesus felt very close to his heart that Easter night while having dinner with his disciples.

Then, on that Easter night, the Lord Jesus while sitting at the table with the Twelve, in fulfillment of the prophetic words of Simeon, presented Himself as the Lamb of God. Jesus Christ was the Messiah; He was that child who hoped That Simeon would save mankind from its sins. In the Upper Room there in the beloved city, Jerusalem, Jesus was there, surrounded by his disciples a few hours after the Redemption were consummated, that is, a few hours after Jesus, like the Passover Lamb, was sacrificed to give freedom from sin.

The Evangelist Luke says that: "There was also a prophetess named Anna, daughter of Penuel, of the tribe of Aser. She was already very old. She married when she was very young and had lived with her husband for seven years; she had been a widow for eighty-four years. He never left the temple, but served the Lord Day and night, with fasts and prayers. Hannah introduced herself at that very moment and began to thank God and to speak of the baby Jesus to all who awaited the liberation of Jerusalem".[63]

The Jews longed for liberation from Roman power, and yet it was there, among them, the one who could give them the best freedom, the freedom of which the prophesied Anna

---

[62]   Footnote commentary on *the Schematic Study Bible*. (Brazil. United Bible Societies. 2010), 1493

[63]   Luke 2:36'38, (DHH).

had mentioned, although, apparently from biblical history, the inhabitants of Jerusalem either did not understand the prophecies of Simeon and Anna or, did not accept them as valid for their personal interests.

C.- *Different menu.* According to the account in the book of Exodus, the menu on that Passover night was roasted lamb meat and bitter herbs. The divine indication was: "They shall eat the meat that same night, roasted on the fire and accompanied by bitter herbs and unleavened bread".[64] The reason they ate the meat of the lamb accompanied by bitter herbs was, "To remind them of the bitter life they had as slaves in Egypt (Ex 1:14, JV)".[65]

Apparently, the menu of the Passover Supper in which Jesus Christ participated was a little different. It is believed that: "This dish contained a sauce made from fruits, vinegar and spices, and in it the bread was dipped before eating".[66] This is why Jesus had said, "While you were at the table, eating, Jesus said to you, 'I assure you that one of you, who is eating with me, is going to betray me. They became sad, and began to ask him one by one, "Will it be me?" Jesus answered them, "He is one of the twelve, who is dipping the bread on the same plate as me".[67]

Over time, the Jewish Passover holiday has been somewhat modified, because in our time, in Jewish tradition, the Passover menu differs a little from the two nights of Passover: that of Egypt and in which Jesus Christ participated. In Jewish tradition: "On the first night of Passover a family dinner called *Pésaj* of séder is celebrated. The Passover seder dinner consists

---

[64] Exodus 12:8, (NIV).
[65] Footnote commentary on *the Schematic Study Bible*. (Brazil. United Bible Societies. 2010), 114.
[66] Footnote commentary on *the Schematic Study Bible*. (Brazil. United Bible Societies. 2010), 1434.
[67] Mark 14:18-20, (DHH).

of making a meal in which traditionally unleavened bread or matzah is eaten, which was fed by the Hebrews during their journey in the desert, in addition to other dishes, such as lamb's leg, boiled egg, bitter herbs, among other things, and several toasts are made. At the table, moreover, there is always a cup and an extra place for the prophet Elijah".[68]

D.- *Different purpose.* Egypt's Passover was for a liberation from the power of the Egyptian empire. At that time, the Israelite slaves took a lamb from the herd and kept it at home for four days. The Bible says that God instructed Moses and Aaron to tell the entire community of Israel that, "... on the tenth day of this month you will all take one lamb per family, one for each house. If a family is too small to eat a whole lamb, they should share it with their closest neighbors, taking into account the number of people they are and the portions of lamb that are needed, according to what each person has to eat. The animal that is chosen can be a lamb or a kid of one year and without defect, which they will take care of until the fourteenth of the month, the day on which the community of Israel in full will sacrifice it at nightfall".[69]

Apparently, each family or groups of families killed in their homes the lamb they had selected from the herd four days before Easter Night. He was killed on the evening of the fourteenth day of the month of Nisan *at nightfall.* That same afternoon, already at dusk, they roasted it and ate it accompanied by bitter herbs. It was a very long night, no one slept that night, after dinner, the people heard the cries and cries of the Egyptian neighbors because their firstborn sons, at midnight were killed by *the destroyer – The wounder –*."[70]

---

[68] Meanings: *Meaning of Passover: Passover Seder.* (La Habra, California. Internet. Retrieved July 14, 2021), ¿? https://www.significados.com/pascua-judia/

[69] Exodus 12:3-6, (NIV).

[70] Exodus 12: 23, (DHH).

The purpose of that first Passover in Egypt was to put an end to Egyptian slavery and to bring the Israelite people out of the empire that had them enslaved to take them to a land where milk and honey flowed; it was a land that God promised them as their new homeland. The Jewish Passover was, then, a political and social liberation.

At the Passover that Jesus Christ celebrated, he himself was the Lamb of God who had offered himself since before the very creation of the universe as the Redeemer of future humanity.[71] We can say that the Father God chose Jesus from before the foundation of the world so that, on the feast of Paschal, he would be sacrificed for the benefit of humanity, just as the lamb in Egypt was sacrificed to feed and prepare the Israelite people for a trip to a new homeland, likewise, Jesus, was sacrificed in that Passover of the Last Week of life of Jesus on this earth to rescue us from this Evil world and lead us into His Celestial Kingdom.

It was also a very long night; Jesus Christ did not sleep that last night. We do not know exactly what time "the wounder" or the soldiers arrested Jesus and from then on, it was all lament, screams and sadness because of the arrest, the unjust trial made of Jesus and his cruel crucifixion.

So, the purpose of the Last Supper in which Jesus participated in his last earthly Week was to provide eternal salvation for all mankind. Always remembering that, not all "*the chicks stayed in the nest*". That is, although the Redemption made by Jesus Christ is for all mankind, not all is redeemed; only those who believe in Jesus Christ and accept Him as their Lord and Savior of their lives.

---

[71] Ephesians 1:4.

CONCLUSION.

Blessed is the Last Passover Supper in which Jesus Christ participated! There, with these three great questions: I.- Where do you want us to prepare the Passover meal for you? II.- What do the words of Jesus mean when he said: *My time is near*? And III.- What are the differences between the Passover of Egypt and that of Jerusalem? with these three questions we realize that in: The Last Passover Supper, the Lamb of God, who had been chosen since before the foundation of the world WAS BACK THEN and WAS AT THE TIME and IS the Savior of all mankind.

The whole ritual of the Feast of Easter is summed up in one person: Jesus Christ. The Lamb of God who was sacrificed by being hung from a cross so that you and I can walk freely to the Heavenly Homeland.

Now, with greater authority, Jesus Christ, the Lamb of God, says to you, "I am the way, the truth, and the life; no one can go to the Father if it is not through me".[72] Jesus Christ is the only God who has allowed himself to be killed for the good of humanity, therefore, he is the ONLY God who can save you from all your sins.

---

[72]   John 14:6, (NLT).

THE ARREST OF JESUS

"Jesus was still speaking when Judas, one of the twelve, arrived. He was accompanied by a large mob armed with swords and sticks, sent by the chief priests and village elders. The traitor had given them this password: 'Whoever gives him a kiss, that is; drag it.' Then Judas approached Jesus and greeted him.
- Rabbi! He said and kissed him. 'Friend', Jesus replied, 'what are you coming to?'
Then the men came and arrested Jesus".
Matthew 26:47-50

INTRODUCTION.

The Lord Jesus Christ shared a night of fellowship with His disciples that Thursday night of *The Last Week* of Jesus' earthly life. Now, what we are going to hear or read these days is not pleasant at all. It is something bloody and cruel; it is illogical and unfair; it is unpleasant and stormy. Still, it was the Lord's plan to fulfill the ministry of salvation of lost humanity; it was and is the Salvific Plan, made by God Himself.

We understand that: "A crucified Messiah was an anomaly to the common expectations of the Jews, but it became one of the fundamental historical factors in the preaching and teaching of the Early Church. A crucified Messiah may also seem anomalous to modern people, Christian and non-Christian alike, who want a more synthesized kind of 'good news'.[73]

In the last week of Jesus Christ's earthly life, we find the account of his arrest on the Mount of Olives while in the company of his disciples. What we can learn from the texts we have read is that first of all:

I.- ALL AGAINST JESUS CHRIST.

Have you heard the expression "*bullies*"? Well, in the Bible this expression does not appear, but action does. The Gospels narrate very often that the Pharisees, the Sadducees, the scribes, the Essenes and the Herodians, the latter two almost did not do it openly as the Pharisees, the Sadducees and the scribes did, in the accounts of the Gospels, we find them always accompanied, never alone, asking questions or slandering Jesus: They were *bullies*!

Jesus was giving his disciples the last instructions. It was there that he told them that the time had come when the shepherd would be wounded, and the sheep would be scattered. Peter told him that he was not going to be scandalized. I think I can put these words in Peter's mouth: 'Lord, even if everyone abandons you, I will never do it'. Jesus' concrete

---

[73]   Michael J. Wilkins. *Matthew:*". (Nashville, Tennessee. Editorial Vida. 2016), 856.

answer left him with his mouth shut. Peter, tonight you are going to deny me three times.

Now notice what the Bible says: "Jesus was still speaking, when Judas, one of the twelve disciples, arrived accompanied by many people armed with swords and sticks".[74] What is this action called? Whatever you want to call it, but I call it: *bullies*! Judas with many people against one called Jesus.

Did you notice it? The Bible says that Judas arrived *accompanied by many people*; that is, they were not soldiers, but townspeople. Why do I say they weren't soldiers? Because the armor they wore were swords and sticks; swords that anyone could carry. Peter, Jesus' disciple, had one. Roman soldiers did not use sticks to fight.

Among those *many people* were the guards of the Temple, who, with all certainty, were the ones who brought the swords. They were the guardians and servants of the high priest. They were all Jews. So, both the temple guards and the unruly men who were surely hired by the high priest were all against Jesus Christ. *bullies*!

Jesus is brought before Pilate, who was the Governor, and who should have sent his soldiers to arrest Jesus, if he had committed any crime. Pilate did not arrest him. He rightly said to Jesus, "Those of your nation and the chief priests are the ones who have given you to me. What have you done?"[75]

What had he done? Preach to them about the truth found in the Scriptures! And by the way, Pilate, like the Jews, also did not want to hear the truth from the mouth of the ONE True God.[76]

Is it possible that Jesus Christ has been imprisoned again, but now in the United States of America? I'm afraid so. We

---

[74]   Matthew 26; 47a, (DHH).

[75]   John 18:35, (NIV).

[76]   John 18:38.

look at the laws on abortion, the freedoms of Santeria and witchcraft; when the "Ten Commandments" have been placed out of reach of the public; when prayer to Jesus Christ has been forbidden in public places and institutions such as schools, even though other groups may pray to their gods in public, it is not ok to pray to Jesus Christ; when the reading of the Bible in government institutions is prohibited; when we have the announcement of churches that will be closed for not complying with the demands of the government; when the possible imprisonment of pastors who refuse to celebrate same-sex marriages is possible; when we hear that the so-called *wise men* of this world say that Christians have a retrograde mind and, when we begin to announce that we must stop preaching about sin and its disastrous effects. When we see and hear all this, it can be said that They have arrested Jesus Christ again!

II.- "DON'T LET HIM ESCAPE".

My father was a very introverted person. In his way of being, when visitors came to our house, if my brother Israel or I spoke very loudly or we ate very quickly in front of the visitors, very sneakily, without saying a word, he would beckon us. We had to abide by the sign because otherwise we knew that when the visit left, we would receive the appropriate punishment.

Judas Iscariot apparently also liked to beckon without speaking. He said to his companions to the Garden of Gethsemane: at my sign. "Judas, the traitor, had given them a password, telling them, 'Whoever I kiss, that is; drag it'."[77]

---

[77]   Matthew 26:48, (DHH).

Judas' command was, *first of all*: "Do not be confused. To the one I kiss, 'that's it.'" Judas had plenty of time to plan the arrest of his Master. It was night, so it would be very likely that the rabble would make a mistake and take some of the disciples while Jesus escaped. The other possibility, it seems, is that Judas did not want the arrest of his friends, his goal was to arrest Jesus so that his purpose would be fulfilled. Judas wanted Jesus to start a kind of Civil War so that the Kingdom of God could begin, there in Jerusalem.

I could say that his expression, *"Let him not escape"*, was with good intention. Not all good intentions are "good", sounds silly. Not everything you think is good for you, your family, your church, or your pastor is good. When Dr. John F. Hall was studying at the School of Medicine, one of the exams featured a question that said, "Is the insecticide good or bad for flies?" His answer was that it was good. Wrong answer. His teacher told him, "It's not good, it kills them!" Not every good intention is good.

Second, Judas says to lovers of cruelty, "Drag him out". Judas, who had walked with Jesus in different places, knew he could escape. He had already done it on other occasions. It is possible that Judas remembered the incident at Nazareth. One day Jesus came to his village. "Generally, Jesus was welcome in Galilee (Luke 4:15), but in Nazareth he was rejected, and they even wanted to kill him".[78] That day, he entered the synagogue of Nazareth, read them the passage from Isaiah 61:1-2, and then said that on that day the Scripture was being fulfilled. After a short speech, listeners were angry at what they were hearing. The biblical account says, "Hearing that, the people of the synagogue were furious. They jumped up,

---

[78] Commentary on *the Schematic Study Bible*. (Brazil. United Bible Societies. 2010), 1498

attacked him and forcibly led him to the edge of the hill on which the city was built. They wanted to throw him off the cliff, but he passed through the crowd and went on his way".[79]

So, what we see in Judas' action is that: "with the kiss, I was not only trying to identify him, but also to hold him back enough so that those who came with him could safely catch him".[80]

III.- TAKEN PRISONER TO GIVE US FREEDOM.

On the Mount of Olives, where Jesus and his disciples were, that night of his arrest, when the people who arrested him arrived, something extremely interesting happened; something that only John recorded. When the people approached Him, Jesus asked them, "Who are you looking for?" "We are looking for Jesus of Nazareth", they told him. Jesus' response was, "I am Him". When Jesus said this answer, the aggressors "retreated, and fell to the ground".[81]

When they stood up, Jesus said again, "I have already told you that I Am Him.... Since I am the person you are looking for, let the others go." Their minds were so blinded by hatred that they didn't realize Jesus was in full control; He could have run away in front of them. It was night and Jesus had friends who could hide him. A friend lent him the donkey to enter Jerusalem, another lent him the Upper Room to celebrate Passover. So, another or some of them could hide him from the persecutors. But he didn't! Jesus did not escape! Jesus had a plan and a ministry to fulfill. He made himself a prisoner; he let himself be trapped to give us freedom.

---

[79]   Luke 4:28-30, (NTV).
[80]   Matthew Henry. *Matthew: Exegetical-devotional commentary on the entire Bible.* Td. Francisco Lacueva. (Terrassa (Barcelona), Spain. Editorial CLIE. 1984), 516.
[81]   John 18:4-6

"All His steps during the last days make it very clear that Jesus gave His life, and that no one took it from Him. Jesus did not die because men killed Him, but because He chose to die".[82] Why did he do it? Notice what the biblical account continues to say: "He did it so that his own words would be fulfilled: 'I did not lose a single one of those you gave me'."[83] "Jesus willingly accepted His death",[84] to give us freedom from sin and death.

From this incident arises the following question: Who are free from any guilt of sin? "Only those he makes free are free".[85] Jesus Christ said, "So if the Son makes you free, you are truly free".[86] These were words that offended the Jews, who, despite having been slaves in Egypt; slaves of the Philistines, Canaanites, and Amorites; slaves in Babylon and, in Jesus' time, slaves in Rome, yet they said they were free.

Cyril, one of the sages of Jerusalem, said that Joseph was sold to be a slave, but he was free, all radiant with nobility of the soul. You may think you're free, but if you're practicing something routine, you're a slave to it! In speaking to them of freedom and slavery, Jesus was referring to sin, to the practice of sin. "He who commits sin, he told them, is a slave to sin".[87] Jesus paid the ransom price from that bondage. He became a prisoner for us.

[82] William Barclay. *Commentary on the New Testament: Volume 2: MATTHEW: II.* Trd. Alberto Araujo. (Terrassa (Barcelona), Spain. Editorial CLIE. 1997), 405

[83] John 18:9, (NIV).

[84] William Barclay. *Commentary on the New Testament: Volume 2: MATTHEW: II.* Trd. Alberto Araujo. (Terrassa (Barcelona), Spain. Editorial CLIE. 1997), 405.

[85] Matthew Henry. *Matthew: Exegetical-devotional commentary on the entire Bible.* Td. Francisco Lacueva. (Terrassa (Barcelona), Spain. Editorial CLIE. 1984), 517.

[86] John 8:36, (NTV).

[87] John 15:13, (NTV).

CONCLUSION.

Even though everyone is against Jesus, he remains in control of the situation. Jesus Christ will never escape what He must do in order to protect us. Christ Jesus has taken our place; He allowed Himself to be imprisoned so that we would be free.

That Jesus allowed Himself to be arrested was within His Redeeming plan. Let us remember that he had said, "The Father loves me because I give my life to receive it again. No one takes my life, but I give it of my own free will. I have the right to give it and to receive it again. This is what my Father commanded me".[88] So Jesus' arrest has another great lesson for us: His Great Love! He later confirms this truth when he said, "There is no greater love than giving one's life for one's friends".[89]

Ah, my beloved brothers and sisters! Jesus Christ, there, on the Mount of Olives, in that Garden of Gethsemane, our Lord and Savior, allowed Himself to be arrested for his love for us. For this and much more, Jesus Christ; He is our Redeemer!

Amen!

---

[88]   John 10:17-18, (DHH).
[89]   John 15:13, (NTV).

THE SILENCE OF JESUS

"Then when the chief priests and elders presented their accusations against him, Jesus was silent. - Don't you hear all the accusations against you? Pilate asked. To the governor's surprise, Jesus did not respond to any of those charges".

Matthew 27:12-14, (NLT).

INTRODUCTION.

When God is silent it is terrifying. What to do when we have no apparent response from God? We pray, ask and plead and even quote biblical passages and God seems to be so far away from us that He does not listen to us.

The composer and singer, Prieto Sánchez Oriol, in his song entitled: El Silencio de Dios, says:

"Crying out to heaven I seek an answer
For this feeling, for that orchestra conductor
How to tell you if you never answer me?

If sometimes I think I see you, what attention do you pay to me?

Mansions and palaces hold centuries of wealth
Your purity is stained, I wanted to see you
on that shore when you prayed
Fruit of anguish and nerves
And the only thing that comes is the silence of God".[90]

Ah, the silence of God! Have you ever wondered why God is silent? In this case, in the presence of the Governor Pontius Pilate, Jesus was silent because he was inside the:

I.- PROPHETIC FULFILLMENT.

Although some human beings bump into the wall because of prophecies. One thing is very certain; The prophecies about the Messiah Jesus Christ were made by God and it is God Himself who fulfills them. Even in spite of the unbelief of the human race; God fulfills what He prophesies! When the Lord says He's going to do something. He does it! He does not need permission to do it. When He said through the prophet Isaiah that the Messiah would close His mouth to the accusations and blasphemies of His enemies, God Himself fulfilled It in the person of Jesus Christ.

Isaiah's prophecy says, "Battered and humiliated, he did not even open his mouth; as a lamb, he was taken to the

---

[90]   Prieto Sánchez Oriol. *The Silence of God.* (La Habra, California. Internet. Retrieved March 5, 2021), ¿? https://www.google.com/search?q=el+silencio+de+dios&rlz=1C 1GCEA_enUS764US764&oq=El+silencio+de+Dios&aqs=chrome.0.69i59j 46j0l8.12327j0j15&sourceid=chrome&ie=UTF-8

slaughter; like a sheep, he was silent before his shearer; and he didn't even open his mouth".[91]

In his arrest, Jesus is brought before the religious authorities. So: "Official circles have tried Jesus and found him guilty of blasphemy, for which he is sentenced to death".[92] However, like them, they do not have the authority to impose the death penalty, they bring him before Pilate, not to judge him, but to issue the death sentence. In other words, Jesus Christ never had a right judgment; the religious leaders of Jerusalem had decided to kill him and for this, they invent a ridiculous judgment; a trial full of lies, saturated with religious hatred, and a trial against the Talmudist tradition.

The Jewish leaders accused Jesus of blasphemy. But this accusation was not valid as a death sentence among the Romans. So, in order to present Jesus to Pilate for a death sentence, they had to invent three accusations that accredited the death before the Roman authorities.

The first accusation was that Jesus was a revolutionary; this one did have validities, although it was a lie. Many had revealed themselves against Rome and had been executed. In the story we find the Maccabees, Jewish men who rebelled against Rome and were executed.

The second accusation was that Jesus told the people not to pay taxes; it was also a valid accusation, although it was also a lie, Jesus never did such a thing, on the contrary, he told Peter to pay the taxes.[93]

---

91   Isaiah 53:7, (NIV).
92   Michael J. Wilkins. *Bible Commentary with Application: MATTHEW: From the Biblical Text to a Contemporary Application.* (Nashville, Tennessee, USA. Editorial Vida. 2016), 871.
93   Matthew 17:27.

The third accusation was that Jesus presented himself as a king. This one was also valid, although this was a half-truth. Jesus was the king, but he never said he was, he always presented himself as the Son of man or as the Son of God or as the Servant of the Lord.[94] But not as a king, although he said that one day he would establish his kingdom. This was why his response to Pilate, when asked if he was king, was, *"You say so"*.[95] Being a Jewish king was against the laws of the Romans. He would be regarded as an invader over Roman power.

So, they invented "three political accusations, conscious lies, because they knew that these were the only ones that could force Pilate to act".[96] And Jesus, who knew everything that had happened, was silent. A Sovereign Silence to such a degree that "the governor (Pontius Pilate) marveled very much".[97]

Even today, the Sovereign Silence of God leaves us with our mouths open; leaves us thoughtful; it leaves us with an unknown to reflect on our behavior; even today, that silence of God leaves us soaked in a great blessing as we fulfill every prophecy: He, Jesus Christ, closed his mouth so that we may open it and publish that even in the Silence of God, the Lord is in control!

II.- HE REMAINED SILENT IN THE FACE OF FALSE ACCUSATIONS.

This is the second time Jesus has appeared before Pontius Pilate. According to the biblical account: "First, Jesus appears

---

94   Mark 2:10-11; 8:31; Luke 9:22; Matthew 3:17; John 1:14; 14:13; Mark 6:7; 10:45; 14:62
95   Matthew 27:11, (KJ, 1960).
96   William, Barclay. *Commentary on the New Testament: Volume 2: MATTHEW: II.* Trd. Alberto Araujo. (Terrassa (Barcelona), Spain. Editorial CLIE. 1997), 412.
97   Matthew 27:14, (KJ, 1960).

before Pilate (27:2, 11-14), then is sent to Herod Antipas (only in Luke 23:6-12) – who mocked Jesus – and finally presents himself a second time to Pilate, who condemns him to death (Matt. 27:15-26)".[98]

In all that supposed judgment that Pilate made of Jesus, it can be noted that the Sovereign Silence of Jesus controlled the courtroom. He had already done so in the false and repugnant judgment before the high priests Anas and Caiaphas. Notice what Scripture says: "Standing up, the high priest said to Jesus, 'Are you not going to answer? What do these allegations mean against you? But Jesus remained silent. So, the high priest insisted, I command you in the name of the living God to tell us if you are the Christ, the Son of God".[99]

Ah, the Blessed Silence of Jesus! The professor and philosopher Alfonso López Quintás says that we revolve around four levels or realities of life.

1st. Level or reality: objects. This is the value we place on things and thoughts.

2nd. Level or reality: People. This is where the creativity of the arts and cultural works lies. For which we pay huge amounts for, such as a new cell phone.

3rd. Level or reality: Values. At this level is values, such as love, forgiveness, happiness, faith, purity and hope.

4th. Level or reality: Religion. This is the level of the encounter with God. We all confront God at any given time.[100]

---

[98]   Michael J. Wilkins. *Bible Commentary with Application: MATTHEW: From the Biblical Text to a Contemporary Application*. (Nashville, Tennessee, USA. Editorial Vida. 2016), 871.

[99]   Matthew 26:62-63, (NIV).

[100]   Alfonso López Quintás. *"The deep gaze and silence of God."* (La Habra, California. Internet. Retrieved March 5, 2021), ¿? https://www.youtube.com/watch?v=AKeNmX5vfUI

Each level has an answer, a logic and a reality. For example, when we talk about the Fourth Level; In this case, we find ourselves with the silence of God. At the level of religion, what does this Blessed Silence produce for us? It is a silence that increases faith and passion toward Christ the Redeemer. Their silence tells us that God respects our privacy; Why? Because he wants us to love him willingly.

In that divine silence we noticed that Jesus could perform any miracle at that instant, He was not limited of His miraculous powers, and yet Jesus never performed a miracle in His defense, but what He did was out of love for others. The Lord never defended Himself from false accusations out of love for you and me. You know what? This is puzzling!

I must keep silent for some words you say and for some things you do because I love you? This is puzzling to some! That you must keep silent some things you know because you love God and his pastor? This is also puzzling to others!

More disconcerting is when we can almost hear Jesus Christ say, "I trust the Father, for He is love by excellence. And that's why He was silent!"

Ah, Blessed Silence of Jesus! He was never scandalized by the Father. And you know what? God the Father gave credence to Jesus' silence; He resurrected him on the third day! The Lord did not do it for revenge, but He did it out of love for you and me, For the love of humanity!

Now, beware! God never told us He would deliver us from pain. This suffering, sometimes we experience it within the Silence of God. Jesus experienced the emotional and physical pain as he listened to his accusers and felt the blows of his interrogators. But even in that instant, he was silent. This is puzzling!

III.- HE REMAINED SILENT BEFORE THE CONFUSED AUTHORITY.

The third divine action we notice in this biblical account is that Jesus was silent in the face of false accusers. "Pilate was accustomed to prisoners cowering in his presence, and he was surprised that Jesus did not utter a word to those who testified against Him".[101] I have already commented on the prophecy of Isaiah 53:7, for here is Jesus before Pilate doing precisely what the prophecy says. Jesus fulfilled exactly everything written about Him. Jesus stood before Pilate, at that time, his judge. "We could not stand before God because of our sins if it were not for Christ being made sin for us. He was prosecuted so that we would be acquitted".[102]

What, then, is it that we notice in this short, but very significant story? We note that, "Jesus has answered Pilate's initial question and does not need to add anything else; therefore, he does not answer the fabricated charges, and the governor is filled with amazement'."[103] Pilate could not comprehend the Sovereign Silence of the one in front of him.

Jesus knew that: "His hour had come, and He submitted wholeheartedly to the will of the Father".[104] Pilate was urged to answer, but Jesus had told the Father in his prayer in Gethsemane; "Not what I want, but what you want".[105]

---

[101] Charles F. Stanley. *Bible Principles of Life*. (Nashville, Tennessee, USA. Nelson Group. 2010), 1097

[102] Matthew Henry. *Exegetical-Devotional Commentary on the Entire Bible: Matthew*. Td. Francisco Lacueva. (Terrassa (Barcelona), Spain. Editorial CLIE. 1984), 534.

[103] . Michael J. Wilkins. *Bible Commentary with Application: MATTHEW: From the Biblical Text to a Contemporary Application*. (Nashville, Tennessee, USA. Editorial Vida. 2016), 872.

[104] Matthew Henry. *Exegetical-Devotional Commentary on the Entire Bible: Matthew*. Td. Francisco Lacueva. (Terrassa (Barcelona), Spain. Editorial CLIE. 1984), 535.

[105] Matthew 26:39, (NIV).

Yes, there come those moments that, although we are face to face with God, He does not say anything! His Sovereign Silence fills us with amazement. It's those moments when we ask him: God, why don't you give me the answer I expect? Lord, where is your power that the Scriptures flaunt? Lord, did you save me and then ignore me?

I believe that Pilate's attitude helps us to answer these questions. In the biblical account we do NOT read that Pilate was angry that he did not have an answer that urged him; He had to pass a sentence and Jesus did not blame himself or defend himself. Jesus' silence increased the bewilderment. What should I do? I was amazed at the silence of Jesus.

While he was in that critical and wonderful situation at the same time, he gets a message from his wife telling him to have nothing to do with that man. Wow, his wife had not helped much! And yet, as Jesus continues in silence, "the governor is filled with amazement".[106]

Ah, our finite mind and troubled feelings that cannot understand or hear god's silence! Jesus knew that the judgment was a farce and was not willing to play along. If you know that when you are accused, is a false accusation; Be silent! Silence covers mouths and leaves the accusers in a bad place. The centurion and the other soldiers who were caring for Jesus during the crucifixion, seeing and feeling the effects of Jesus' death; "They were terrified by the earthquake and everything that had happened".[107] Within that terror or horror they were experiencing, they recognized the one they had crucified, and then, "They said, 'This man was truly the Son of God!'".[108]

Too late! Jesus had fulfilled the Holy Scriptures. Part of these Scriptures say that now is the time of salvation that "the

---

[106]   Matthew 27:14, (NIV).
[107]   Matthew 27:54a, (NLT).
[108]   Matthew 27:54b, (NTV).

'right moment' is now. Today is the day of salvation".[109] Don't expect to be saved another day, maybe it's too late. Today, Jesus Christ puts his silence aside and says to you, "Come, let's set the record straight, says the Lord. Are their sins like scarlet? They will be white as snow! Are they red like purple? They will look like wool!"[110]

Jesus' silence was to forgive your sins and mine.

CONCLUSION.

"Pilate was a man who felt the power of Jesus – and was afraid to submit to Him. There are still people who are afraid of being as Christian as they know they should be",[111] and with their attitude they deliver Jesus to their enemies.

"Pilate looked for a way to evade his responsibility".[112] And you can do the same, even though you know very well that God's silence does not allow you to evade your responsibility to draw near to God.

The silence of Jesus Christ tells you and me that Jesus is willing to do anything because He loves us, even though you and I do not accept responsibility for God's truth.

So, I end with these questions: What are you going to do when God is silent? Will you despise him? Will you wait for an answer? His silence remains a blessing for humanity. Why not reciprocate that Sovereign silence? In silence, draw closer to Him.

---

[109]   2 Corinthians 6:2c, (NLT).

[110]   Isaiah 1:18, (NLT).

[111]   William, Barclay. *Commentary on the New Testament: Volume 2: MATTHEW: II.* Trd. Alberto Araujo. (Terrassa (Barcelona), Spain. Editorial CLIE. 1997), 412.

[112]   William, Barclay. *Commentary on the New Testament: Volume 2: MATTHEW: II.* Trd. Alberto Araujo. (Terrassa (Barcelona), Spain. Editorial CLIE. 1997), 413.

SUPERLATIVE SUFFERING

"Then they braided a crown of thorns and placed it on his head, and in his right hand they put a reed on it. Kneeling before him, they sneered saying, Hail, king of the Jews!"
Matthew 27:29, (NIV). (27-31)

INTRODUCTION

The account presents that Matthew speaks of the sarcastic mockery with which the Roman soldiers were angry with Jesus of Nazareth. "Sarcasm is a scathing mockery that is intended to imply otherwise or express displeasure".[113] During the last week of Jesus' earthly life, among all the things and activities of the Lord, we have noted that he was imprisoned on the Mount of Olives, and that he was silent before Herod Agrippa and Pontius Pilate.

Now, in the passage we have read from the Gospel of Matthew we notice that in those last days and hours of *The Last Week* of Jesus, walking on this earth, the people of the Palace, the religious leaders, the soldiers and the Jewish

---

[113] Wikipedia, the Free Encyclopedia. *Sarcasm*. (La Habra, California. Internet. Retrieved March 10, 2021), ¿? https://es.wikipedia.org/wiki/Sarcasmo

people, mocked Him: It was sarcastic mockery and brutal beatings with their fists, with whips, with thorns and any object that was found at hand. They were mockery and blows that brought him a Superlative Suffering.

In this type of punishment given to prisoners, some of them fainted before the punishment ended and others died because of the brutality with which the punishment was applied before being crucified. However, to fulfill all the prophecies, Jesus Christ endured all suffering.

So, this morning let me tell you about three lessons that I can see in the account of Matthew 27:27-31, which refers in a few words to the Superlative degree of Jesus' Suffering.

I.- NO APPARENT ESCAPE.

The biblical account says that: "The governor's soldiers took Jesus to the palace and gathered the whole troop around him".[114] As the worst and most cunning criminal, Jesus was led to the palace of the governor Pontius Pilate. Matthew says that Jesus was taken to the governor's barracks *surrounded by the whole company.* "The Greek word translated 'company' can also be translated as *'troop'* or *'cohort'.* This is a battalion of about 600 soldiers".[115] It was probably not the 600 soldiers in charge of torturing Jesus, for, in Pilate's service, there were 120 soldiers. Surely, these were the mockers and torturers of Jesus Christ. 120 against one! What does this action remind you of? How they were also *bullies*!

This reminds me of the night the bell rang announcing the end of classes that day at José María Morelos y Pavón High School, in the city of Morelia, Michoacán, Mexico. I

---

[114]   Matthew 27:27, (NIV).
[115]   *Schematic Study Bible.* (Brazil. United Bible Societies. 2010), 1438

went outside like any of the other nights. At the corner of Calle Carpinteros de Paracho and Avenida los Arcos, one of the rival gangs was waiting for me. Without warning, they surrounded me and, in a few minutes, left me lying at the foot of a small palm tree; I was bleeding, but senseless. I woke up at about four in the morning with pain, cuts and bruises on different parts of my small body. They were also *bullies*!

Well, on that morning, back in the city of Jerusalem, the soldiers gathered "around Jesus to have fun with him. They wanted to satisfy their sadistic impulses. They wanted to have some fun at the expense of the 'King of the Jews'."[116]

1. There were 120 soldiers, they thought that Jesus had no escape.
2. The truth was that Jesus did not set out to escape.
3. He had prayed that the will of the Father would be done, and, in addition, he had said: "That is why the Father loves me: because I give my life to receive it again. No one takes it from me, but I hand it over of my own free will. I have the authority to deliver it, and I also have the authority to receive it again. This is the commandment I received from my Father".[117]

Jesus, although he was in a superlative degree of suffering, did not escape the torturers. He suffered everything so that you and I:

First: Would make sure of God's Great Love for us.

---

[116]   William Hendriksen. *The Gospel of Matthew: Commentary on the New Testament.* (Grand Rapids, Michigan. Distributed by T.E.L.L. Subcommittee on Christian Literature. 1986), 1005.
[117]   John 10:17-18, (NIV).

Second: That we would trust in what God's Word says, that God's Messiah would go through all these sufferings out of love for you and me. His Word is the truth of yesterday, now and forever!

Third: Jesus suffered the superlative punishment so that you and I would not suffer in the hell of fire but would enjoy the Heavenly Abodes.

So: "When you think of the suffering of Christ do not cry for Him, as if pitying or feeling sorrow, for He was going strong and victorious towards the cross to win the greatest battle that could have been in the universe, if you cry do it for you because you are unworthy of such holy and sublime love with which He loved you and cry more if you have not yet known that love".[118]

II.- HELLISH CRUELTY.

When the governor Pontius Pilate handed Jesus over to the soldiers, in addition to beating him: "They braided a crown of thorns and placed it on his head, and in his right hand they put a reed on him. Kneeling before him, they sneered saying, 'Hail, king of the Jews!'."[119] It is not known for sure what kind of thorny plant the soldiers used to weave the crown they put on Jesus' head. Some botanists suggest that it was probably a branch of a plant called "*Spina Christi*

---

[118] D.S.H. *Comment on the Facebook page of the Indigenous Educational Center of the city of Córdoba, Veracruz. Mexico.* (La Habra, California. Internet. Comment published on April 10, 2020. Retrieved August 26, 2021), ¿? https://www.facebook.com/centroeducativoindigena/

[119] Matthew 27:29, (NIV).

or *Palinro* Shrub".[120] When we notice the hellish cruelty with which they treated Jesus, it doesn't matter where they cut off the branch they weaved to put over Jesus' head. What really matters is the significant fact of that crown of thorns.

What we know from the biblical account is that: "Thistles and thorns are mentioned in Genesis 3:18 in connection with the fall of Adam. (So, then), Here in Matthew 27:29, and its parallels, Jesus presents himself carrying the curse on nature in order to free nature and us from it".[121]

In the mockery made by the soldiers, soaked in hellish cruelty, they put on him the crown that they considered worthy of a Jewish king. They used the reed they had given him as a scepter to hit him on the head, and thus cause him more pain by sticking the thorns in his head. "Would those who bothered him understand that they were doing this to the one who is King of kings and Lord of lords?"[122]

The hellish cruelty with which Jesus was treated that morning before he was crucified has no name. Both popular writers, philosophers and biblical writers, claim that the punishment that Jesus received "was a cruel and ignominious punishment, especially when he was executed by the Romans, who were not subject to Judaic law, in which the punishment was moderated, not allowing to pass from forty scourges, even thirty-nine, in case the account failed (2 Co. 11:24)".[123]

Hellish cruelty! Wow, when sin hardens the heart of the human being is degraded much lower than the animals

---

[120] William Hendriksen. *The Gospel of Matthew: Commentary on the New Testament.* (Grand Rapids, Michigan. Distributed by T.E.L.L. Subcommittee On Christian Literature. 1986), 1006

[121] Guillermo Hendriksen. *El Evangelio de Mateo: Comentario al Nuevo Testamento.* (Grand Rapids, Michigan. Distribuido por T.E.L.L. Subcomisión Literatura Cristiana. 1986), 1006-1007.

[122] Deuteronomy 10:17; Psalms 136:3; 1 Timoteo 6:15; Revelations 1:5; 17:14; 19:16; 19:11-16.

[123] Matthew Henry. *Exegetical-Devotional Commentary on the Entire Bible: Matthew.* Td. Francisco Lacueva. (Terrassa (Barcelona), Spain. Editorial CLIE. 1984), 540.

themselves! It turns into a deranged beast! And yet, William Barclay suggests that everything the soldiers did with Jesus, was "acted in ignorance".[124] My respects to Barclay, but I doubt it. Jesus was not the first or the last to be tortured. They knew what they had done! You and I know when we are acting worse than animals against a fellow human being. We are not innocent! Nor ignorant of what we do.

III.- THE AMAZING LOVE OF CHRIST HUMBLES US.

The mockery, someone said: "Mockery is the means used by the self-conscious ignorant to feel wise".[125] But, the great geniuses of Universal History did not use mockery as a weapon either to amuse themselves or to humiliate human beings. What can be noticed in these great geniuses is humility.

Jesus, the man who "like a lamb was taken to the slaughterhouse" without resistance, with his amazing love teaches us that:

A.- Thinking that acting in ignorance, as William Barclay suggests, when the soldiers acted with hellish cruelty against Jesus, has justification. The sarcastic thing is that ignorance does not spare responsibilities. If you drive at 100 miles per hour on a road and the signs mark 70 miles maximum speed and you are stopped by the police and you allege that you

---

[124]   William Barclay. *Commentary on the New Testament: Volume 2: MATTHEW:* II. Trd. Alberto Araujo. (Terrassa (Barcelona), Spain. Editorial CLIE. 1997), 419.

[125]   @nochedeletras. *Mockery of God: Phrases.* (La Habra, California. Internet. Retrieved March 10, 2021), ¿? https://www.google.com/search?rlz=1C1GCEA_enUS764US76 4&hl=en&q=La+burla+hacia+Dios&tbm=isch&chips=q:la+burla+hacia+dios, online_chips:frases&usg=AI4_-kTCq0zoeAAQLezuuK_9EEx3-

didn't know the speed limit, that doesn't save you from the fine and possibility of going to jail.

When you die and stand before God because we will all stand before Him. The Bible says, "... each person is destined to die only once and then the judgment will come".[126] As this is a natural law, unless Jesus Christ returns in our day, we will all die and all stand before the Lord. And when you come before God and he tells you that the only way to be with Him is to have accepted Jesus Christ as your personal Savior and you tell the Lord that you didn't know, your ignorance will not allow you to be with God for eternity. So, make sure you can live with God for all eternity.

B.- The astonishing love of Jesus teaches me that "I am forced to humble myself".[127] This humiliation is to "accept any suffering that crosses my path in order to advance God's purposes in my life".[128]

C.- The humiliation of Jesus "shows me, in a unique way, a whole New Dimension".[129] In these pandemic days when COVID-19 vaccines are being applied, there is talk of a New World. That is nothing new.

1. The Egyptians, the Chaldeans, the Persians, the Greeks, even the Isrealites when they crossed the

---

[126] Hebrews 9:27, (NLT).

[127] Michael J. Wilkins. *Bible Commentary with Application: MATTHEW: From the Biblical Text to a Contemporary Application.* (Nashville, Tennessee, USA. Editorial Vida. 2016), 917.

[128] Michael J. Wilkins. *Bible Commentary with Application: MATTHEW: From the Biblical Text to a Contemporary Application.* (Nashville, Tennessee, USA. Editorial Vida. 2016), 917.

[129] Michael J. Wilkins. *Bible Commentary with Application: MATTHEW: From the Biblical Text to a Contemporary Application.* (Nashville, Tennessee, USA. Editorial Vida. 2016), 917.

river Jordan and they entered Palestine, they all talked about a New World.

2. When Emperor Constantine put Christianity as the imperial religion there was talk of a New World.
3. During the Protestant Reformation and catholic Reforms there was talk of a New World.
4. Before World War 1 there was talk of a New World.
5. After World War 2 there was talk of a New World.
6. Some of you remember that in the last quarter of 1999 there was talk that the end of the world would end in the year 2000. It's not over!
7. Now, in these times, a New World is mentioned again...

The Superlative Sufferings of Jesus DO NOT SPEAK OF A NEW WORLD, but of a NEW DIMENSION.

1. they talk about passing from death to eternal life.
2. they talk about loving instead of hating.
3. they talk about being peaceful instead of loud.
4. they speak of living a life in a dimension of holiness.
5. They talk about God loving you intensely!

Ah, the love of Jesus Christ! He suffered and endured the mockery so that you and I might learn, in humility, to resist suffering and mockery in this Dimension of Love.

CONCLUSION.

When you feel cornered, by the enemy, when you feel hellish cruelty on the part of human beings, think of the love of Jesus. Humble yourself before Him. He has already gone through this suffering. The Lord will not let you go through a Superlative Suffering, you will not be able to endure it, God knows that that's why He took your place.

Now, what are you going to do with all that blood spilled in the Palace of Governor Pontius Pilate? What are you going to do with the love that Jesus Christ has for you? What are you going to do with the humility that Jesus showed to his mockers? Will you continue to mock Jesus Christ and His Word? What are you going to do?

I invite you to repeat with me this prayer:

Lord Jesus Christ, thank you for suffering in my place.

Lord, on some occasions I have felt cornered by the enemy, and I have not found the way out, today, I realize that you are the way out.

Lord, on some occasions I have reacted negatively to the criticism and mockery that has been made towards me, today, Lord, I understand that I must be humble because you have something better for me.

Lord, thank you very much for your love! Thank you because you love me!

I pray in the name of Christ Jesus.

Amen!

IN THE "PLACE OF THE SKULL".

"When they arrived at a place called Golgotha, (i.e., "Place of the Skull"), they gave him to drink wine mixed with ice; but Jesus, after tasting it, did not want to drink it".
Matthew 27:33-34, (DHH).

INTRODUCTION.

Some events of the last week of Jesus Christ's earthly life are: Jesus was arrested on the Mount of Olives while he was praying with his disciples in the Garden of Gethsemane. At night, he was tried in the house of Caiaphas, the high priest of that time.[130] In the morning he was brought before the Roman governor Pontius Pilate, who allows Jesus to be tortured and then delivers him to be crucified.

"And as if the crucifixion were not of its own and a horrible death, - the soldiers, the people, the priests and the thieves who crucified with him – they added – to his crucifixion – all kinds of abusive treatment"[131] I invite you to discuss a little

---

[130] Matthew 26:57.
[131] Matthew Henry. *Exegetical-Devotional Commentary on the Entire Bible: Matthew.* Td. Francisco Lacueva. (Terrassa (Barcelona), Spain. Editorial CLIE. 1984), 543.

what Matthew 27:27-54 says. Let us note three great lessons in this account by the Evangelist Matthew of the crucifixion of Jesus in the *"Place of the Skull."*

I.- NOTE "SAD AND IRONIC".

The Bible says that when Jesus was crucified, in the "Place of the Skull," they placed "... above his head... a sign, where the cause of his conviction was written. The sign read, 'THIS IS JESUS THE KING OF THE JEWS'."[132] This is a note that "picks up an accusation that is the truth: This is Jesus, the king of the Jews. It was a note announcing to all observers that the person who was dying, hanging on that huge cross, was the person who had fed them; He was the person who had healed them; he was the person who had delivered them from the demonic forces; He was the Savior of their souls!

To reach that pitiful but prophetic state, Jesus, born into poverty, was born under the cruel world dominated by Herod the Great. During his ministry he faced Satan's attacks in his constant temptations. Nature also attacked him with a storm. The demon-possessed harassed him more than once. Israel's religious leaders hated him to death.[133]

What we note in New Testament scripture is that: "Jesus continually fought against powerful forces in his mission to establish the kingdom of God".[134] None of them overcame him: Although in an ironic and burlesque way, Jesus, on the cross in the *"Place of the Skull"*, even with the crown of thorns on his head, his sign nailed on the top of the Cross

---

132   Matthew 27:37, (DHH).
133   Matthew 2:1-23; 4:1-11; 8:23-27; 8:28-34; 12:22-45.
134   Michael J. Wilkins. *Bible Commentary with Application: MATTHEW: From the Biblical Text to a Contemporary Application.* (Nashville, Tennessee, USA. Editorial Vida. 2016), 916.

that said: 'THIS IS JESUS THE KING OF THE JEWS', both symbols, announced that Jesus of Nazareth WAS and IS the Lord of the universe. "He was and still is the King of kings and Lord of lords!"[135]

There, in *"The Place of the Skull"*," symbol of hopeless death, Jesus Christ died to give us hope of life. And eternal life!

II.- SACRIFICIAL LOVE.

When the Lord Jesus Christ delivered His message on the true vine, He told His disciples, "The greatest love one can have is to lay down one's life for one's friends".[136] Years later, the apostle Paul said to the brethren of the city of Ephesus, brethren, "... lead a life of love, just as Christ loved us and gave Himself for us as an offering and fragrant sacrifice to God".[137]

Ah, God's love! The love of Jesus Christ that we see reflected in an ironic way in the *"Place of the Skull"*, is not understandable, although it is wonderful. Some of the songs that I learned and that we sang in that small Christian Church of my town; Lombardía, Michoacán, about 60 years ago, but which is still a song that is taught to children and that from time to time we sing in our cults, says:

> "God's love is wonderful.
> God's love is wonderful.
> God's love is wonderful.
> So great is God's love!

---

[135] Revelation 17:14, (KJV, 1960).
[136] John 15:13, (DHH).
[137] Ephesians 5:2, (KJV, 1960).

So high that I cannot be above Him.
Deep that I cannot be below Him.
So wide that I can't be outside of Him.
So great is God's love!"[138]

Yes, very big! In the Seventh-day Adventist Hymnal, there is a hymn that starts with the following lyrics and reads:

"Oh, God's love!
your immensity, man will not be able to count,
nor to comprehend the great truth:
that God could love man.

Choir:

O god's love!
sprouting you are, immeasurable, eternal,
by the ages will last inexhaustible rapids.

If it were ink all the sea,
and all heaven a great role,
and every man a writer,
and each sheet a brush,
to write of their existence,
they would never be enough".[139]

Singers, poets, writers, philosophers, mathematicians, scientists, authors, theologians, historians and even workers,

---

[138]   Album, song and lyrics. *Love is Wonderful.* (La Habra, California. Internet. Retrieved March 17, 2021), ¿? https://www.albumcancionyletra.com/el-amor-de-dios-es-maravilloso_de_ninos___188816.aspx

[139]   Seventh-day Adventist Hymnal. *Oh, God's love.* (La Habra, California. Internet. Retrieved March 17, 2021), ¿? https://www.letras.com.br/himnario-adventista-del-septimo-dia/nos-veremos-junto-al-rio#top=himnario-adventista-del-septimo-dia

speak of the love of God: They speak of that sacrificial love shown to a superlative degree in the "place of the Skull"! There, where the Redemption of humanity took place.

The Chilean philosopher, Luís Gastón Soublette, in an interview said that "Jesus was a very dangerous rooster, and he also said: "The essence of the Gospel of Jesus Christ is very dangerous for power and for these times".[140] I ask myself: Why is "the essence of the Gospel of Jesus Christ so dangerous"? I think it is because it demands humility; demands simplicity; Demands to love!

The religious people of Jesus' time knew this. He knew that Jesus' teachings were very dangerous to their ideals, so they decided to kill him, not realizing that Jesus was in control of the situation because his time had come, they acted, soaked in hatred and with a spiritual blindness that they could not see a small truth of Jesus' teachings. They allowed themselves to be enveloped by sin and sin totally blinded them to the truth that proclaimed and showed the love of God in the person of Jesus Christ.

They, because of sin, could not see the love of God in the "Place of the Skull": There, where the symbol of death was, they did not realize that there was the opportunity to be new people; They did not realize that there, in that place of death, they could have eternal life.

Beware! you can be in the "Place of the Skull"; you may be contemplating God's love for you; you can be present before the same Savior of your soul, and you may still understand the sacrificial love of Jesus Christ! So let me tell you right now that: If someone really loves you, that's Jesus Christ! His crucifixion, in the "place of the Skull," was because he loves you.

---

[140] Video. *"La religión ha ocultado a Jesucristo"* ... - Jesucristo Cambia. (La Habra, California. Internet. Entrevista en un canal de televisión chilena. Publicado el 27 de noviembre dl 2019. Consultado el 18 de marzo del 2021), ¿? https://www.facebook.com/watch/?v=442931106409060

III.- THE "MANTLE OF SIN" OVER THOSE PRESENTS IN THE "PLACE OF THE SKULL".

Part of the Evangelist Matthew's account of the hours that Jesus of Nazareth was hanging on the cross in the *Place of the Skull* says: "The people who passed by shouted insults and moved their heads mockingly. ' But look at yourself now! They shouted at him. You said you were going to destroy the temple and rebuild it in three days. All right, if you are the Son of God, save yourself and get off the cross.' Chief priests, teachers of religious law, and elders also mocked Jesus. 'He saved others,' they mocked him, 'but he cannot save himself! Didn't he claimed he was the King of Israel? Let him come down from the cross right now and we will believe in him! He trusted God, then, may God rescue him now if he wants to! For he said, 'I am the Son of God'.' Even the revolutionaries who were crucified with Jesus mocked him in the same way".[141]

An impressive story! Now, what can we notice in this paragraph of Matthew 27:39-44? In a quick and concise manner, let us note three great lessons that evangelist Matthew bequeathed to us in his gospel:

A.- *Mockery, insults, contempt, slander, hatred and everything that comes from an evil and ungrateful heart is what was seen and heard in the "Place of the Skull".* This was on the part of most of those present. The other side of the coin showed that there in the *Skull Place,* God's love was pouring out to lost humanity. The apostle Paul said, "But God shows his love for us, in that, while we were still sinners, Christ died for us".[142]

141   Matthew 27:39-44, (NTV).
142   Romans 5:8, (KJV, 1960).

Simply put, the apostle Paul tells us that "we have hope because God loves us in Christ".[143] It is a love that stands out within all the Mockery, the insults, the contempt, the slander, the demonic hatred of those minds and those evil hearts. It's total love. That is to say: "God does not distribute his love in droppers: he 'has poured it out' ... – everything – into our hearts".[144]

B.- *Covered with sin.* The darkness that appeared in the "Place of the Skull" for three hours, of which I will mention in another message, is a symbol of the sin that surrounded the people; a symbol that prevented them from seeing God's love through his Son; it was a symbol of the sin of mankind that Jesus Christ was carrying upon Himself. But even there, amid all that blackness of sin, those closest to Jesus' noticed something terrifying and at the same time sublime. With much fear, for they were terrified of what was happening in the "Place of the Skull," while Jesus was dying, the Roman centurion and the soldiers present publicly confessed who the person they were murdering was, "... And they said, Truly this was the Son of God".[145]

The biblical account we have read: "It is an impressive picture for readers of Matthew. The catastrophic events that Matthew mentions testify to the true identity of Jesus, and the centurion and his men take a step of faith to recognize the truth of this testimony".[146] This is the only way to recognize who exactly Jesus of Nazareth is. You can hear all year round about Jesus and his wonders or his teachings, but if you don't approach Jesus and take a step of faith to truly confess what

---

[143] Douglas J. Moo. Romans: *Commentary with application; from the biblical text to a contemporary application.* (Miami, Florida. Editorial Vida. 2011), 164.

[144] Douglas J. Moo. *Romans: Commentary with application; from the biblical text to a contemporary application.* (Miami, Florida. Editorial Vida. 2011), 164.

[145] Matthew 27: 54c, (KJV, 1960).

[146] Michael J. Wilkins. *Bible Commentary with Application: MATTHEW: From the Biblical Text to a Contemporary Application.* (Nashville, Tennessee, USA. Editorial Vida. 2016). 909.

you are feeling or seeing, you will never truly know the identity of Jesus Christ.

Amid all your sins, if you approach Jesus, in the *Place of the Skull,* in that place, you will find the Savior of your soul; there, in that symbol of death, you will find the true love that will give you eternal life.

C.- *Sacrificial love justifies.* Apart from the women and the disciple John at the foot of the cross, the rest were so blind and stubborn in their beliefs that they could not see the love of God in the Person of Jesus Christ.

So, in the worst circumstances surrounding Jesus on the Calvary: "Matthew narrates... a peaceful, if melancholic, scene of the women who have faithfully observed the unfolding events".[147] They are not unaware that the one who is crucified is the Son of God; they are not unaware that out of love for humanity, Jesus is laying down his life. The love that Jesus had shown towards them prevents them from running out of that terrifying scene; their commitment to the love of Jesus keeps them firm on the Calvary.

What could we call the courage and determination of these women? According to the Gospels, they had followed Jesus from Galilee. Someone who follows a teacher is called a disciple. And: "A 'disciple' is someone who has assessed the cost, made a commitment of faith, and then followed Jesus".[148] Does the example of these women tell you anything? Yes, it seems to me that it tells you that, if you have made a commitment of love to Jesus Christ, you must stand firm in

---

[147] William Hendriksen. *The Gospel of Matthew: Commentary on the New Testament.* (Grand Rapids, Michigan. Distributed by T.E.L.L. Subcommittee on Christian Literature. 1986). 1012

[148] Michael J. Wilkins. *Bible Commentary with Application: MATTHEW: From the Biblical Text to a Contemporary Application.* (Nashville, Tennessee, USA. Editorial Vida. 2016). 909-910.

the "Place of the Skull". Why there? Because from that place, your victory against sin and Satan is certain.

What we know from the Bible itself is that the love that was manifesting itself there, in the *Place of the Skull*, was and is a justifying love. The apostle John said, "The Blood of Jesus Christ cleanses us from all sin".[149] "Napoleon said...... That the laws were for ordinary people, but not for people like him".[150] You can say that you do not need to be justified from your sins; you can say that the love of God manifested in the "Place of the Skull" is not for you, and yet, if you are an honest man, if you are an honest woman, you know you need to be loved!

CONCLUSION.

So, there, in the "Place of the Skull", in that mortal chaos, the love of God was manifested amid not to great of circumstances. No matter what circumstances you find yourself in, God's love will be with you.

But much more important is that there on the Calvary, in that place called "of the Skull," the Savior of the world gave his life because he loves you and wants to save you. "After all, Scripture does NOT place all the emphasis on what Jesus suffered physically, but on the fact that He Himself, in His body and soul, was made a sin offering and laid down His life",[151] so that you and I may be saved from our sins.

Jesus Christ loves you!

Amen!!!

[149] I John 1:7, (KJV, 1960).
[150] William Barclay. *Comentario al Nuevo Testamento: Volumen 15: 1ra, 2da, 3ra de Juan y Judas*. Td. Alberto Araujo. (Terrassa (Barcelona), España. Editorial CLIE. 1998), 41.
[151] Guillermo Hendriksen. *El Evangelio de Mateo: Comentario al Nuevo Testamento*. (Grand Rapids, Michigan. Distribuido por T.E.L.L. Subcomisión Literatura Cristiana. 1986). 1012.

THE GOODNESS OF JESUS

First Word: The Merciful Word:
"Jesus said, 'Father, forgive them, for they
do not know what they are doing".
Luke 23:34, (DHH).

INTRODUCTION.

In chapter 27 of the Gospel of Matthew we note that, in those last days and hours of The Last Week of Jesus, walking on this earth, the people of the Palace, the religious leaders, the soldiers and the Jewish people, mocked Him and tortured Him with different blows. It was a sarcastic mockery and brutal blows with fists, with whips, with thorns and any object that was found at hand. They were mockery and blows that brought him a Superlative Suffering.

Now, following the biblical account, it is Friday. On this day, very early, or rather, at dawn, Jesus is arrested and brought before the Sanhedrin that was led by the priests Anas and Caiaphas. After an unjust religious trial, he is sent to the governor Pontius Pilate. Pilate sends him with the corrupt and unhinged Herod Antipas who returns him to Pilate because Jesus did not fulfill his miraculous desires.[152]

In the Palace of Pontius Pilate, Barabbas appears, the despised character, the individual who was the scum of the Palestinian territory. To Pilate's question of whom he should set free, the immediate answer was: To Barrabas! This was a custom among the Jews, on the day of Passover a prisoner was released. At that time, Barrabas is free, and Jesus is the victim. "Barrabas was released; to imply that Jesus was condemned so that the greatest sinners might be acquitted; he was given so that we might obtain freedom".[153] The apostle Peter said that "Christ died for sins once for all, *the righteous for the unjust*".[154] On that Friday morning of Jesus' Last Week on this earth, God's Messiah is sentenced to death by governor Pontius Pilate, there, it was once again shown that the Holy Son of God died for everyone regardless of their social or sinful status. He died even for the most despised and hated of human beings as Barrabas was in his time.

There was no escape anymore. Jesus was taken to the place of the Skull, he was hung from the cross, his sufferings and pains were a Superlative Suffering. It was there that the last six hours of his earthly life began. There, too, the last seven expressions of the one who WAS and IS the Lamb of God who takes away the sin of the world were heard. That is, the one who WAS and IS the Jewish Passover Lamb.

The incomprehensible thing about this terrible scene is that the first thing the crucified one said was a plea to the Great God and Heavenly Father. It was a plea for kindness. Amid

---

[152] *Jesus is arrested*: Matt 26:47-56; *Jesus is taken to the Jewish Council*: Matt. 27:57-67; *Jesus is brought before Pilate*: Matt. 27:1-2, 11-14; *Jesus stands before Herod Antipas*: Luc. 23:6-11.

[153] Matthew Henry. *Comentario Exegético-Devocional a toda la Biblia: Mateo.* Td. Francisco Lacueva. (Terrassa (Barcelona), España. Editorial CLIE. 1984), 540.

[154] I Peter 3:18, (NIV). The **bold** and *Italics* are mine.

his sufferings and pains that were Sufferings of Superlative degree, he asked the Father to forgive those who had caused him that evil.

So, his first expression from the cross was:

**"FATHER, FORGIVE THEM, BECAUSE
THEY DON'T KNOW WHAT THEY DO".
Luke 23:34, (RV, 60).**

Wow, what a short prayer, but with a passion and theological depth that is difficult to understand! Within the most terrible cruelty that the human being can do to his fellowmen, Jesus intercedes so that his annoying and cruel accusers may be forgiven. Incomprehensible!

Now, for whom does he intercede before the Heavenly Father? It is very likely, firstly, that Jesus asked the Heavenly Father to forgive:

I.- THE GOVERNOR'S SOLDIERS.

The evangelist Matthew says about the activity of the soldiers under the command of the governor Pontius Pilate, the following: "The soldiers of the governor took Jesus to the palace and gathered all the troops around him. They took off his clothes and put on a scarlet cloak. Then they braided a crown of thorns and placed it on his head, and in his right hand they put a reed on it. Kneeling before him, they scoffed, saying, Hail, king of the Jews! And they spit on him, and with the cane they hit his head. After mocking him, they took off his cloak, put on his own clothes, and took him away to crucify him".[155]

---

[155] Matthew 27:27-31, (NIV).

Yes, Jesus intercedes before the Father for the governor's soldiers. He intercedes for them even though they were the ones who beat him, it was them who spit on his face, it was them who mocked Him, it was them who crucified him, it was them who gave him to drink vinegar instead of water, it was them who stripped him naked and it was them who distributed within themselves the clothing of Jesus, there, at the foot of the cross.[156]

The biblical account says that the soldiers gave a barbaric treatment to Jesus Christ. Where it should be a refuge from abuse, that is, in the Praetorium itself, there the soldiers abused their authority, they did not respect even the Roman law of waiting for execution, because: "after being condemned, they should have allowed him a little time to prepare to suffer the death of the cross. There was a law, ruled by the Senate of Rome, ordering that the execution of criminals be delayed for ten days from the pronouncement of the sentence. But the Lord Jesus was not allowed even ten minutes of rest. The barbarism against him continued without interruption".[157]

There was no apex of godliness for Jesus Christ! The soldiers acted cruelly and ruthlessly with God's Messiah.

And yet Jesus Christ, from the cross on the Calvary, pleads with the Father to forgive them. This is not understandable to our senses and reasoning!

If we can say anything in favor of the soldiers, it is that they were obeying the governor's order and perhaps, therefore, Jesus said that they did not know what they were doing. Did he justify them? Apparently so. From the point of view of the biblical narrative and story about this fact, there

---

[156]   Matthew 27:34-35.
[157]   Matthew Henry. *Exegetical-Devotional Commentary on the Entire Bible: Matthew.* Td. Francisco Lacueva. (Terrassa (Barcelona), Spain. Editorial CLIE. 1984), 540.

was no reason for the soldiers to be justified, much less for Jesus Christ to show goodness to them. But he did!

¡Oh my, the mysteries of God!

II.- JESUS INTERCEDED FOR THOSE WHO CONDEMNED HIM.

Literally, in that historical moment, there on the Calvary, Jesus asked the Father to forgive the soldiers because they didn't know for sure who they were crucifying. For them, he was just one more inmate who had to die crucified on the orders of the governor.

However, by extension of the historical moment, we can say that the expression of Jesus: *"Father, forgive them, because they do not know what they are doing"*,[158] reached to encompass the main protagonists of that historical moment. From the agony of the cross, Jesus prays to the Father that he also forgives:

A.- Pontius Pilate. This character was: "Roman Governor of Judea remembered in history as an anti-Semite with a horrible reputation, and in Christian creeds as the magistrate under whose power Jesus Christ suffered (I Tim 6:13). The NT calls him 'governor', while other sources call him 'procurator' or 'prefect' (Inscription found in Caesarea in 1961)".[159] As governor, one of the cases he had to deal with was the request for death for Jesus of Nazareth in the early years of his governorship. Pilate began to rule Judea around 26 DC, and about 30 DC. Jesus Christ stood face to face before him.

As governor, he questioned Jesus before the accusers. After Pilate's first interrogation of Jesus, Pontius Pilate

---

[158]   Luke 23:34, (KJV, 60).
[159]   S. Leticia Calcada. (General Edition). *Holman Illustrated Bible Dictionary.* (Nashville, Tennessee. B and H Publishing Group. 2008), 1278.

realized that Jesus was innocent. The biblical account says that: "Pilate gathered the chief priests, the authorities, and the people, and said to them, 'You brought this man to me, saying that he stirs up the people; but I have questioned him in front of you and I have not found him guilty of any of the faults of which he is accused'. Nor has Herod, for he has given it back to us".[160] But because of the insistence of the Jewish leadership, Pontius Pilate returned: "For the third time - to the people and - he said to them, 'For what evil has he done? I find nothing in him that deserves the death penalty. I'm going to punish him and then set him free'."[161] "Pilate testified repeatedly and forcefully about the innocence of Christ (Luke. 23:4, 14, 15). In doing so, he not only condemned the Jews, who demanded the death of Jesus, but also himself, because he gave up the Savior for no reason".[162]

Pilate knew that Jesus was innocent and for that reason, from that moment "he tried to set Jesus free, but the Jews shouted uncontrollably: If you set this man free, you are not a friend of the emperor. Anyone who pretends to be king becomes his enemy".[163]

The accusation of the Jews was: "We have discovered this man stirring up our nation. He opposes paying taxes to the emperor and claims that he is the Christ, a king".[164] But Pilate did not find that this accusation was true.

However, although he found no guilt in Jesus, the insistences and threats of the religious and political leaders of the Jewish people frightened the governor, and Pontius Pilate

---

[160] Luke 23:13-15, (DHH).

[161] Luke 23:22, (DHH).

[162] John Macarthur. *A Perfect Life: The Complete Story of the Lord Jesus.* (Nashville, Tennessee. Nelson Group Inc. A registered trademark of Thomas Nelson Inc. 2012), 452.

[163] John 19:12, (NIV).

[164] Luke 23:2, (NIV).

did not have the courage to exercise his Roman authority over the desires of foolish Jews "and surrendered Jesus to their will".[165]

Despite this attitude of Pontius Pilate, bribed by the Jewish people, Jesus interceded before the Father God to forgive him.

B.- To the Sanhedrin, that is, to the Pharisees and Sadducees. Also, for this political-religious group, Jesus asked for God's goodness toward them. The Sanhedrin was a: "Supreme Jewish Council of the first century, it had 71 members and was preceded by the high priest. Among its members it included the two most important parties",[166] – Pharisees and Sadducees-.

It was they who gave the order to arrest Jesus while he was in the Garden of Gethsemane with his disciples. They arrested Jesus at night, probably at dawn, between five or six in the morning, at that time they took him before the high priest Anas who made a fraudulent judgment. In the morning, when the Sanhedrin had already met, they made another trial, one more formal but just as fraudulent. In both cases they decided to fulfill their desire to kill Jesus.[167] "Criminal proceedings were considered illegal if they were carried out at night, so the Sanhedrin waited wisely until dawn to issue the verdict that in any case had already been agreed".[168]

Thus, the Sanhedrin, after a very fraudulent judgment, sentenced Jesus, saying, "He is guilty, and he must die".[169]

---

[165] Luke 23:25, (DHH).

[166] S. Leticia Calcada. (General Edition). *Holman Illustrated Bible Dictionary.* (Nashville, Tennessee. B and H Publishing Group. 2008), 1444.

[167] John 11:45-53.

[168] John MacArthur. *A Perfect Life: The Complete Story of the Lord Jesus.* (Nashville, Tennessee. Nelson Group Inc. A registered trademark of Thomas Nelson Inc. 2012), 445

[169] Matthew 26:66, (DHH).

The truth is that they were to blame because in their desire for revenge, in their desire to remove from their presence the one who performed miracles in the name of God and in their anger against the Nazarene who called himself the Messiah of God, they decided to kill him. They were the culprits, and they were the ones who deserved to die! However, in the goodness of Jesus Christ, he begs forgiveness for them, saying, *"Father, forgive them because they don't know what they do".*

C.- To the people who asked for him to be crucified. The soldiers of the governor, Pontius Pilate and the Sanhedrin took Jesus like a lamb to the slaughterhouse. But Jesus alone was brought that way, but the Jewish leaders also led the people to a spiritual sentence; they were led to shout, *"Crucify him! Crucify him!"*[170] without them remembering that many of them had received or witnessed one or more miracles, without remembering that many of them were fed with the loaves and fishes that Jesus had multiplied.[171]

For them, for those who allowed themselves to be deceived, Jesus also begged forgiveness for what they had done, saying, *"Father, forgive them because they do not know what they are doing".* Jesus intercedes for those who are led by religious and political leaders who call evil good and good bad. And that, at the end of the day, they don't know what they're doing.

The goodness of Jesus Christ is unlimited, whatever we do, knowingly or unknowingly, Jesus Christ continues to intercede with the Father, saying, *"Father, forgive them because they do not know what they do".*

So, when Jesus said that first expression from the unbearable pain of the nails that held him hanging from that

---

[170]　　Luke 23:20, (NIV).
[171]　　Matthew 14:13-21.

rustic wooden cross, the pain of the thorns of that crown on his head, and of a heart hurt by the bestial acts of those whom he came to save, his expression of intercession for those who did not know exactly what they were doing, it is incomprehensible.

What we come to understand is that this request for forgiveness was the beginning of one of the beautiful ministries of the Crucified and Risen One; Christ Jesus: Intercedes! The elderly apostle John, in his first letter to the Christians of his time, told them: "My dear children, I write these things to you so that you may not sin. But, if anyone sins, we have before the Father an intercessor, Jesus Christ, the Just One. He is the sacrifice for the forgiveness of our sins, and not only for ours, but for the whole world".[172]

This Johannine text introduces the third point of reflection on the petition of Jesus Christ when he said: "—*Father...,*
forgive them, for they do not know what they are doing"[173].

III.- JESUS INTERCEDED FOR US.

Let us note once again the words of the apostle John: "My dear children, I write these things to you so that you may not sin. But if anyone sins, we have before the Father an intercessor, Jesus Christ, the Just One".[174] The elder John, with these words, is saying "that there is forgiveness for sins in what Jesus Christ has done and continues to do for mankind".[175] That is to say that the extension of the intercession made on the Calvary has reached our time; Jesus Christ continues to intercede before the Father to forgive us.

---

[172]   1 John 2:1-2, (NIV).

[173]   Luke 23:34, (NIV).

[174]   1 John 2:1, (NIV).

[175]   William Barclay. *Commentary on the New Testament: Volume 15: 1st, 2nd, 3rd John and Jude.* (Terrassa (Barcelona), Spain. Editorial CLIE. 1998), 48.

As I have said before, the goodness of Jesus Christ has no limit, it has reached the twenty-first century with this work of intercession: "Father, forgive them because they do not know what they do." Jesus Christ is still the Advocate! He is our Advocate before the Father God!

When the apostle John speaks of us as a lawyer who is Jesus Christ, "it is the same Greek word that appears in John 14:16, 26; 15:26; 16:7, and which translates to 'Comforter', in a context in which the Holy Spirit is spoken of".[176] The term Comforter, "in the Greek text – is - Parakletoς - a term that – literally has the meaning of someone who is called to come to the side. In the context he is called to help in a situation of great difficulty",[177] such as when we sin knowingly or when we sin by being deceived either by Satan or by leaders with evil intentions.

In addition, the word *Comforter* also means "helper, supporter, and above all witness of someone, lawyer in the defense of someone".[178] When Jesus Christ spoke the words of intercession: *"Father, forgive them because they do not know what they are doing"*, not only was he and still is, helping the sinner to recognize his sin, but even more, as he knows that we have sinned consciously or unconsciously, that is, he is a witness before God that we sin, then he becomes our advocate. His great goodness moves him to the point of saying to the Righteous Father, *"Forgive them, for they do not know what they are doing"*.

Now, as Christians, then, we have a double blessing: Jesus Christ is interceding for us before the Father God begging

---

[176]   Commentary on *the Schematic Study Bible*. (Brazil. United Bible Societies. 2010), 1875.

[177]   Samuel Perez Millos. *Exegetical commentary on the Greek text of the New Testament: John.* (Viladecavalls (Barcelona), Spain. Editorial CLIE. 2016), 1354.

[178]   William Barclay. *Commentary on the New Testament: Volume 15: 1ˢᵗ, 2ⁿᵈ, 3ʳᵈ John and Jude.* (Terrassa (Barcelona), Spain. Editorial CLIE. 1998), 50.

him to forgive our sins and at the same time, he is in the Holy Spirit who accompanies us to comfort us and help us not to continue sinning.

So, the intercession of Jesus Christ from the Calvary when He said, *"Father, forgive them because they do not know what they are doing"*, is still effective on our behalf.

CONCLUSION.

"Father, forgive them because they do not know what they are doing," is a statement of intercession that only Jesus Christ can fulfill, for it was the Lord Jesus who paid the price of sin. In our contemporary world, Jesus Christ continues to intercede. He did it for the soldiers, he did it for Pontius Pilate, and he also did it for the members of the Sanhedrin and for the Jewish people of his time. Now he does it for us; you and I are included in that kind intercession. Jesus intercedes for us because still in the twenty-first century, incredibly, we don't know what we are doing with God!

Today, Jesus is interceding for you and me because when we sin against God, when we sin against our neighbor, and even when we sin by being deceived, the words of intercession on our behalf resonate strongly on the Heavenly Throne and in the heart of God. And the Father God, forgives us!

Jesus Christ continues to intercede for us with these words of kindness: *"Father, forgive them because they do not know what they are doing"*.[179]

¡Amén!!!.

---

[179] Luke 23:34, (NIV).

RECOGNITION OF THE PROMISED MESSIAH

The Second Word: The Word of Hope –
"I assure you that today you will be with me in paradise."
Luke 23:44, (KJV,60).

INTRODUCTION.

The scene that we are contemplating in a historical way about the events of Mount Calvary, is not pleasant at all.

The athlete called: The Canarian D.C., a young man of 39 years who practiced sports five times a week, who was "fond of boxing and who cared about good nutrition, spent possibly the worst eight days of his life in the ICU – in the Hospital -, where there were times when he thought about the possibility that he could die. When he stopped being sedated and regained consciousness he realized where he was: unable to breathe and with a 'tremendous fear'."[180]

---

[180] Belén Rodríguez (EFE). *"Please get vaccinated,"* says a 39-year-old from Tenerife and athlete *from the hospital.* (La Habra, California. Internet. Article published on August 5, 2021, at 11:27 h. Retrieved August 19, 2021), ¿? https://www.diariodepontevedra.es/articulo/espana/favor-vacunense-dice-tinerfeno-39-anos-deportista-hospital/202108051127151153780.html

This young man, like many others, is one of those who had not been vaccinated against COVID-19. Repentant for not getting vaccinated, while outside the hospital he said: "'In the ICU you see pretty hard things; there were people who were very bad next to me', said the young man, who acknowledged that he felt panic because he did not know if he was going to improve or not, since his lungs 'were very bad'."[181]

Repentant of not being vaccinated, from the hospital he made the following call "to his generation: 'Please get vaccinated'."[182]

The scene presented to us by the historian and evangelist Luke also looks at pretty hard things; It speaks among other things of a person who thought he would never be hanging on a cross in his last hours of life. This person is what he called: *The Crucified Other.* A person who, while in a panic of what would happen to him in the other dimension, called on Jesus of Nazareth to accept him into his Kingdom. It is a plea of panic, but at the same time hopeful: "—Jesus, remember me when you begin to reign".[183] And Jesus gave him good hope! "I assure you that today you will be with me in paradise".[184]

What can we learn from this wonderful and hopeful response from Jesus of Nazareth, the Promised Messiah? Three lessons:

---

[181] Belén Rodríguez (EFE). *"Please get vaccinated," says a 39-year-old from Tenerife and athlete from the hospital. (*La Habra, California. Internet. Article published on August 5, 2021, at 11:27 h. Retrieved August 19, 2021), ¿? https://www. diariodepontevedra.es/articulo/espana/favor-vacunense-dice-tinerfeno-39-anos-deportista-hospital/202108051127151153780.html

[182] Belén Rodríguez (EFE). *"Please get vaccinated," says a 39-year-old from Tenerife and athlete from the hospital. (La Habra, California. Internet. Article published on August 5, 2021, at 11:27 h. Retrieved August 19, 2021), ¿? https://www. diariodepontevedra.es/articulo/espana/favor-vacunense-dice-tinerfeno-39-anos-deportista-hospital/202108051127151153780.html

[183] Luke 23:42, (DHH).

[184] Luke 23:44, (KJV,60).

I.- PUT ON HIGH.

Remember that: "The scene of the crucifixion was in a place called 'the Skull'. His Aramaic name is '*Golgotha*': in Latin, *Calvaria*, which is why we refer to him as the Calvary".[185] The great Moses left this instruction about the person who was judged as a bad person or who was regarded as cursed by God. He said: "If someone who commits a crime worthy of death is convicted and hanged from some wood, you will not leave the body hanging during the night, but you will bury it that same day. Because anyone who is hanged... is under the curse of God".[186]

Jesus Christ, who never committed a single sin was treated as the worst criminal in Jewish history, although, He WAS and IS innocent! "Pilate, Herod and a criminal – the crucified Other – confessed the innocence of Jesus".[187] And yet, they caused him one of the most horrific deaths. The death on the cross was one of the most horrific tortures of that time and I think it still is; thirst, hunger and gangrene accelerated the death of the crucified.

In addition to being a cruel death, what we notice from the Scripture and ecclesiastical history is that Jesus was hung from a higher cross than was customary, the reason being for him to die asphyxiated by not being able to breathe because of gravitation. He was also crucified on high so that the text I have already quoted from Deuteronomy 21:22-23 would be fulfilled. Because according to this text, those they considered cursed, were hung higher so that the perverted would not contaminate the earth with his wickedness.

---

[185] Darrell L. Bock. *Bible Commentary with Application: LUCAS. From the biblical text to a contemporary application.* (Miami, Florida. Editorial Vida. 2011), 543
[186] Deuteronomy 21:22-23, (NIV).
[187] Darrell L. Bock. *Comentarios Bíblicos con Aplicación: LUCAS. Del texto bíblico a una aplicación contemporánea.* (Miami, Florida. Editorial Vida. 2011), 544,

Certainly some, such as B. H. Carroll do not believe that Jesus' cross was taller than that of thieves, however: "According to an ancient tradition, the Cross of Jesus Christ measured in length very close to 189 inches (4.80 meters), from 90.5 to 102.5 inches (2.30 to 2.60 meters)".[188] Tall enough for the soldier who gave him to drink vinegar to use a reed to get the sponge with vinegar to Jesus' lips.[189]

In addition to this, Jesus was raised in prophetic fulfillment that gave Jesus a Recognition that He was the Promised Messiah. The sign they placed above Jesus' head, the apostle John says that "this sign was written by Pilate himself, a message that was intended to be ironic. For a king, stripped naked and executed in public, obviously had to have lost his kingdom forever. But Jesus, who inverts the wisdom of the world, thus began his kingdom. His death and resurrection would deal a mortal blow to Satan's rule and establish his eternal authority over the earth".[190] Jesus, WAS and IS the Messiah Promised by God to save mankind!

II.- MOCKERY TOWARDS THE INNOCENT.

The servant of God, that is, Jesus Christ, said the prophet Isaiah that: "He was a man full of pain, accustomed to suffering. As someone who does not deserve to be seen, we despised him, we did not take him into account.... though he never committed any crime nor was there deception in his

---

[188] Ken Graham. *How much did the Cross of Jesus weigh?* (La Habra, California. Internet. Article published on April 8, 2021. Retrieved August 19, 2021), ¿? https://www.actualidadcristiana.net/cuanto-pesaba-la-cruz-de-jesus/

[189] Mark 15:36.

[190] Raul Araque. *The sign on the Cross.* (La Habra, California. Internet. Retrieved August 19, 2021), ¿? https://apuntesteologicos78.blogspot.com/2017/02/el-letrero-en-la-cruz.html

mouth".[191] Jesus Christ WAS and IS innocent! Therefore, we must follow the thoughts of the crucified Other who recognized that Jesus of Nazareth was the Messiah of God: The Messiah Promised to the Jewish nation!

Now, what can be noted in Scripture is that: "Luke develops the account of Jesus' crucifixion through his interaction with a series of observers",[192] The soldiers, the religious leaders, some of the Jews, the women who followed Jesus to the Calvary, and John the beloved disciple, all of them were watching every movement, every gesture and every feeling of pain of the Crucified One, Christ Jesus. That is to say that there on the Calvary: "... there are a lot of people. The crowd that demanded his execution has stayed to see how it is carried out. Within the crowd was a group of women, mourning his suffering and imminent death".[193]

The preacher and writer B. H. Carroll, classifies the crucifixion observers by class and says that the First Class were the "ones who passed by and said insults to him by shaking their heads and saying, 'You who tares down the temple, and in three days rebuild it, save yourself: if you are the Son of God, descend from the cross'."[194]

About the Second Class, Carroll says they were "the chief priests who also mocked him. They, together with the Scribes, and the elders, saying, 'Others saved likewise cannot be saved! If he is the king of Israel, let him descend now, and we will believe in him! He trusted in God, deliver him now,

---

[191] Isaiah 53:3, 9, (DHH).

[192] Darrell L. Bock. *Bible Commentary with Application: LUCAS. From the biblical text to a contemporary application.* (Miami, Florida. Editorial Vida. 2011), 542

[193] Darrell L. Bock. *Bible Commentary with Application: LUCAS. From the biblical text to a contemporary application.* (Miami, Florida. Editorial Vida. 2011), 542

[194] Carroll, B. H. *Bible Commentary: The Four Gospels. Volume VI. Volume II.* Trd. Sara A. Hale. (Terrassa (Barcelona), Spain. Editorial CLIE. 1986), 451

if he loves him!' These scorners were the members of the Sanhedrin".[195]

Yes, of course, Jesus had saved others, in that these mockers were right. That He was the King of Israel, not only was He King of Israel, but Jesus Christ WAS and IS King of kings and Lord of lords. A King whom the Father God loved and loves with an incomprehensible love so much that, when his Beloved Son was bearing the sins of us all; In sins that disfigured him, the Father hid the face of his Son through a very dense darkness.

that evil heart and with that confused mind, of these classified by B. H. Carroll as mockers, I doubt that if Jesus had come down from the cross, they would really believe in him. Maybe they would accuse him of being a sorcerer or something like that, they would look for any other pretext or heresy not to accept him as the Promised Messiah; not to accept Him as the Lamb who takes away the sins of the world. Accept Him as their Savior? Please let me doubt it!

Among the observers were also the two thieves who were crucified, one to the right and the other to the left of Jesus. This act was in fulfillment of Isaiah's prophecy, when he said that in addition to having voluntarily surrendered to death, he also: "... was counted among the wicked".[196]

Then, in the scene of the Calvary it could be seen that: "Those who passed, the Scribes, the priests, the elders and those who suffered with him, all mocked him".[197] It was there, at that historical moment when the insults and mockery of some of those present towards Jesus Christ were heard, that

---

[195] Carroll, B. H. Bible Commentary: *The Four Gospels. Volume VI. Volume II.* Trd. Sara A. Hale. (Terrassa (Barcelona), Spain. Editorial CLIE. 1986), 451

[196] Isaiah 53:12, (DHH).

[197] Carroll, B. H. *Bible Commentary: The Four Gospels. Volume VI. Volume II.* Trd. Sara A. Hale. (Terrassa (Barcelona), Spain. Editorial CLIE. 1986), 451

a plea from the Other who was crucified together with Jesus is also heard, saying: "Remember me when you come in your kingdom".[198]

This is a plea from someone who, after observing the scene very closely, not only realizes that Jesus is innocent, but recognizes that Jesus of Nazareth is the Promised Messiah. This recognition or repentance of the crucified Other teaches us "that it is never too late to recognize Jesus as our King and Savior".[199]

So, within all the mockery of the innocent Jesus, there is the Recognition that Jesus of Nazareth is the Promised Messiah.

III.- SECURITY FOR THE UNWORTHY.

Since man sinned in the Garden of Eden, God, from right there, began the historical moment of the salvation of mankind. The Bible says that: "God the Lord made clothes out of skins for the man and his wife and clothed them".[200] To make the fur clothes, some animal had to have died, possibly a lamb, the blood was shed to cover the shame of the first couple. On the Calvary, Jesus Christ died to pay the price of sin. His blood was shed on this earth for mankind to achieve forgiveness of sins because He WAS the Promised Messiah, the Lamb of God who takes away the sin of the world.

This Redemptive Work could not be done in all the history of mankind before Jesus Christ. The Leviticus sacrifices announced that the Lamb of God would come to take away

---

[198]   Luke 23:42.
[199]   William Barclay. *Commentary on the New Testament: Volume 4: LUKE.* (Terrassa (Barcelona), Spain. Editorial CLIE. 1994), 344.
[200]   Genesis 3:21, (NIV).

the sin of the world because none of the previous sacrifices managed to take away sin, they only covered it until Jesus showed himself up and voluntarily gave himself up to die for all the sins of the history of the human race.[201]

So, Jesus, God's Messiah: "Being blameless, the only man in all of history who was completely pure and sinless, Jesus, was the only one who could 'stand in the gap,' the only one from whom Satan could not demand anything. He was the only one who did not deserve death, either physically or spiritually speaking. But, for carrying out the purpose for which he had come to Earth, offering Jesus willingly, he was crucified as the last innocent sacrifice. He died as the Lamb of God, to the Atonement of all mankind".[202] This is what the crucified Other recognized and so he begged to enter the kingdom of Jesus Christ.

I repeat, it is interesting to note that among all those mockeries of Jesus Christ, a prayer was heard that was completely different from those heard among the observers and executors of Jesus Christ; It was the voice of the Other crucified, it was the voice of Another crucified who recognizes the greatness of Jesus, it was the voice of One of those who were hanging on a cross that recognizes that Jesus is the Messiah of God and that, therefore, for him, Jesus, is not only innocent, but still has the power to give life beyond the cross on which he is hung.

That crucified Other was someone who for society was worth absolutely nothing: He was a drag on society! He was a criminal! And yet he was someone, by the way, the first in the entire history of salvation in Christ Jesus who asks to

---

[201] John 1:29; 1 John 2:2.

[202] Milenko van der Staal. *Why did Jesus have to die on the cross?* (La Habra, California. Internet. Retrieved August 18, 2021), ¿? https://cristianismoactivo.org/por-que-tuvo-que-morir-jesus-en-la-cruz

be accepted into the Kingdom of God. "And, although the thief – that is, the crucified Other – did admit to deserving the punishment he received for his mistakes (Luke 23:40-41), ... He simply made a positive comment about Jesus Christ, who responded with comforting words referring to the future that awaited him in the Kingdom of God".[203] "I assure you that today you will be with me in paradise".[204] It was Jesus' consoling and eschatological response."

Wow! what an encouraging response! Amid all the pain and minutes before death took over his life, the crucified Other receives a hope that surely allowed him to die trusting in the promise of the Promised Messiah.

Jesus promised the crucified Other that on that same day he would be with him in paradise. "The word *paradise* comes from Persian and means a *walled garden.* When the Persian king wanted to do a great honor to one of his servants, he would name him his companion in paradise, so that he could walk and talk with the king in that delicious place".[205]

So, Pastor, what did Jesus promise the crucified Other? What the Promised Messiah promised to the crucified Other: "It was more than immortality: He promised him the honor of enjoying his company in the garden of the heavenly court".[206] God's Messiah when he promises, he fulfills it! That is to say, the crucified Other was someone of great value to Jesus Christ, because it was to him that the King of kings and Lord of lords did not deny him the entrance to eternal salvation,

[203] Life, hope and truth. *What happened to the thief on the cross?* (La Habra, California. Internet. Retrieved August 18, 2021), ¿? https://vidaesperanzayverdad.org/vida/vida-despues-de-la-muerte/que-es-el-cielo/ladron-en-la-cruz/

[204] Luke 23:44, (,60

[205] William Barclay. *Commentary on the New Testament: Volume 4: LUKE.* (Terrassa (Barcelona), Spain. Editorial CLIE. 1994), 344.

[206] William Barclay. *Commentary on the New Testament: Volume 4: LUKE.* (Terrassa (Barcelona), Spain. Editorial CLIE. 1994), 344

but, in response to his plea, Jesus said to him: "*I assure you that today you will be with me in paradise*".[207]

CONCLUSION.

Our Lord and Savior Jesus Christ was put up hanging from a rustic cross as if telling the world that he was the worst of criminals. Not content with that, the mockery and blasphemy towards the innocent Jesus were heard for hours on the Calvary. Ah, the dark hearts!

And yet, from there, from the top of the Calvary and from the highest cross, Jesus Christ, gave eternal security to the one who was worthless before society. The one without social value came to enter the kingdom of God by the pure grace of Jesus Christ!

My friend, on the Calvary, with the death of God's Messiah, began the blessed Redemption of humanity. This means that, you are not exempt from it, all you must do is exclaim the same supplication of the crucified Other. "—Jesus, remember me when you come into your kingdom".[208] And Jesus, in his blessed grace, will say to you, "*I assure you that today you will be with me in paradise*".[209]

---

[207] Luke 23:44, (KJV,60).
[208] Luke 23:43, (NIV).
[209] Luke 23:44, (NIV).

COMFORT FOR THE HELPLESS AND REJECTED

- Third Word: The word careful –
"When Jesus saw his mother, and at his side
the disciple whom he loved, he said to his
mother, 'Woman, there you have your son.
Then he said to the disciple, "There you
have your mother. And from that moment
that disciple received her in his house.
John 19:26-27, (NIV).

INTRODUCTION.

"It was 9:59 a.m. – on September 11, 2001 – and the second
tower attacked was about to collapse. That was a terrible scene,
everyone ran around trying to save their lives. Sergeant John
McLoughlin also ran, but to help those who were confused
by the rumble. Thinking that the strong beams supporting
the elevator would save them from dying, he shouted to the
desperate looking for shelter as the walls of the tower began

to crumble: 'Run to the elevator! To the elevator pit!' Sgt. John yelled at them.

As he ran, he noticed how the building was collapsing. From one moment to the next: 'The rain of debris threw him to the ground and his helmet flew through the air'. In those circumstances, Sergeant John said: 'I couldn't believe my eyes... It was a total disaster, like a combat zone'."[210]

The scene that the apostle John and the women who loved Jesus there on Mount Calvary saw and experienced was also something they could not believe. They had crucified the innocent Master of Nazareth! They had crucified His Beloved Master and Son!

While John and the women beheld and grieved at such a terrible punishment for which he had done only good to all who had come to him seeking relief from his ills, the Beloved Son, lowers his sight from the Cross and contemplates his mother Mary full of pain and says the most beautiful consoling words that can be said to a mother: Here is your son, fulfilling the purpose for which I came into this world. While he says to John, his beloved disciple, "Take care of her!" she is now your mother.

Yes, on Mount Calvary it was "a total disaster." The Lamb of God, in those terrible hours, was dying to deliver from sin every human being who accepted His offering of forgiveness. What else can we learn from that terrible scene? I invite you to think about three great lessons.

---

[210]   Daniel Rome Levine. *Buried alive*. (New York. USED. Reader's Digest Inc. Selections Section: Achievers. August 2006), 41-42. Note: All sentences or expressions that are in quotation marks were copied verbatim from the writing of Daniel Rome Levine.

I.- THE GOSPEL OF POWER.

The apostle Paul told Timothy to stoke the fire of God's gift.[211] What gift was he referring to? Paul was referring to the Gift of the Holy Spirit, that gift that gives incomprehensible power and love. It is the gift found in the Gospel of Jesus Christ. What I mean is, we speak of the Gospel that "was, and is, power to conquer the ego, power to dominate circumstances, power to continue living when life is unlivable, power to be Christians when being a Christian seems impossible".[212]

Marvelous Gospel of power! That is why the apostle Paul tells Timothy that: "God has NOT given us a spirit of fear, but a spirit of power, of love, and of good judgment. That is why Timothy keeps saying to him, Paul do not be ashamed then, to bear witness on behalf of our Lord".[213]

An example of this courage in being a witness of Jesus Christ is the apostle John and Mary the mother of Jesus. What we can notice in the scene of the Calvary is that, within the whole multitude of mockers, there is one of Jesus' disciples: One! Of all his male followers, only one is present before the Lamb of God who at that time and instant was crucified. While everyone mocked the crucified Jesus, John, the beloved disciple is running the risk of being imprisoned and mistreated and perhaps, even crucified, because "he was always dangerous . . . to be associated with a Person whom the Roman government considered dangerous enough to deserve the cross".[214] But there he remained. This is cause of his love despite of it all!

---

[211]   2 Timothy 1:6.

[212]   William Barclay. *Commentary on the New Testament: Volume 12: Wrath and 2 Timothy, Titus, and Philemon.* (Terrassa (Barcelona), Spain. Editorial CLIE. 1998), 176.

[213]   2 Timothy 1:7-8, (DHH).

[214]   . William Barclay. *Comentario al Nuevo Testamento: Volumen 6: JUAN: II.* (Terrassa (Barcelona), España. Editorial CLIE. 1996), 289.

John made it clear that God had given him a *spirit of power*. This was the disciple who, at Jesus' last supper with his disciples, lay on Jesus' chest. He really loved Jesus and the Lord also him, the Bible says that: "One of them, **whom Jesus loved very much**, was next to him, while they were having dinner".[215]

One day, while Jesus and Peter were walking in dialogue on the beach of the Sea of Galilee, "Turning Peter, he saw that they were followed by the disciple **whom Jesus loved**, the same one who at the supper had lay down next to him, and had said to him, Lord, who is it who is to give you?"[216] Not only was it the love between them, but, in addition, John, had been endowed with a courage that made him face any negative situation. And there on Mount Calvary, it was demonstrated that God had not only given him "a spirit of love" but had also "a spirit of power and courage."

In the middle of that gloomy scenario, you could see a ray of white light, I mean: "In the end, Jesus was not completely alone. Near the Cross were four women who loved Him",[217] and a disciple who also loved Him. John, the beloved disciple, showed a love and courage that he shared and impacted and encouraged Mary, who also stood firm in the company of the other Mary's in the midst of all the threats, criticisms, mockery, insults and blasphemies they heard against His Beloved Son. In addition, it is to be admired "like the weaker sex of women, it seems here more manly, firm by the cross, when the disciples fled".[218] Love casts out fear! So said the apostle, John. [219]

---

[215]   John 13:23, (DHH). The **Bolds** and the *italics* with mine.

[216]   John 21:20, (DHH). The **Bolds** and the *italics* with mine.

[217]   William Barclay. *Commentary on the New Testament: Volume 6: JOHN: II.* (Terrassa (Barcelona), Spain. Editorial CLIE. 1996), 289.

[218]   Saint Thomas Aquinas. Catena Aurea: *Commentaries on the Gospel of John.* (San Bernardino, California. USED. Ivory Falls Books. 2019), 527

[219]   I John 4:18.

One of the strong teachings we notice in the attitude of the women on the Calvary is that: "The eternal love of all mothers was represented in Mary – and the other Mary's – at the foot of the Cross".[220] Ah, how valuable it is that, apart from God, someone else is by your side when you need it most to support and encourage you!

Wow! there is no doubt that the Gospel that the apostle John had heard from the lips of Jesus was a Gospel of power and love! It is that same Gospel that we have today, so even in the worst circumstances, in the unpleasant and dangerous situations, the Spirit of power and love that God has given us is a great shield.

Let us follow the example of John and the other women who accompanied Mary in her grief! Oh, as St. Ambrose said in one of his epistles: "Imitate, pious mothers, this one, who gave such a heroic example of maternal love to her most loving only Son".[221]

II.- THE GOSPEL OF JESUS CHRIST PROVOKES CONJECTURE.

Within the scene of Jesus' crucifixion, two expressions had already been heard that had come out of the mouth of Jesus of Nazareth. The first was, *"Father, forgive them because they don't know what they're doing"*.[222] The second was, *"I assure you that today you will be with me in paradise"*.[223] Now we come across the third expression or statement of the crucified

[220] William Barclay. *Commentary on the New Testament: Volume 6: JOHN: II.* (Terrassa (Barcelona), Spain. Editorial CLIE. 1996), 290.
[221] Saint Thomas Aquinas. Catena Aurea: *Commentaries on the Gospel of John.* (San Bernardino, California. USED. Ivory Falls Books. 2019), 527
[222] Luke 23:34, (KJV, 1960).
[223] Luke 23:43, (KJV, 1960).

Christ Jesus. It was two statements that say, "Woman, there you have your son. And —There you have your mother".[224]

If we emphasize what Jesus said to his mother, we must ask ourselves: Why did Jesus say this expression? And why did his mother commission the beloved disciple? It is here that the Gospel provokes the conjectures. This does not mean that the Gospel of Jesus Christ is not truthful, but simply does not explain why Jesus expressed Himself in this way.

Some of the answers that have been given to these expressions of Jesus Christ are:

1. Jesus put his mother in John's care because Joseph, Mary's husband, had died. This is a probability.
2. Jesus put his mother in the care of John because John was the son of Zebedee and Salome, who was the sister of Mary the mother of Jesus. Therefore, John was a cousin of Jesus. This is also a probability.
3. Jesus put his mother in the care of John because he was the only one who was with Jesus until the last breath of the Crucified.

These conjectures are probable because, according to the Gospel of Mark, Jesus' brothers thought he was crazy. Shortly after Jesus began his earthly ministry he chose his Twelve disciples, Mark says, "Then he entered a house, and again so many people gathered that Him and his disciples could not even eat. When his relatives found out, they went out to take care of him, because they said, 'He's beside himself'."[225] We know that, until after the Resurrection of Jesus, at least two of his brothers accepted the teachings of the Lord: James and Judas.

---

[224]   John 19:26-27, (NIV).
[225]   Mark 3:20-21, (NIV).

We read in the Gospel of John that Jesus' brothers did not believe in Him. The writer said a very regrettable statement: "The truth is that not even his brothers believed in him".[226]

So, Jesus knew that they would not accept their mother who had believed that their Beloved Son was actually the Messiah Promised to the Jewish nation. With this belief, they would most likely not accept her among themselves, consider her a heretic, and being a heretic person at the time, she risked being stoned.[227]

It is very likely that when Jesus said to John, *there you have your mother*, "He wanted John to take care of her. Because Mary's children – were homeless. John had comfort; he was the most well-to-do of the apostles. And for this reason, He would commission John to take care of his mother".[228] This may be the strongest and most reasonable reason why Jesus left his mother in John's care, although, I admit, it remains a guess".[229]

However, even though we don't have the exact explanation of why Jesus said to John, "There you have your mother," we do notice that this is a word that indicates Jesus' care for his mother even in the last moments of his life. He handed her over to the care of someone he knew would protect her. And so: "from that moment that disciple received her in his house."

Mary was not left helpless; Jesus Christ got her a safe place against the contempt of her own children and against the hatred of the Jews. "Jesus entrusted Mary to the care of John, and John to the care of Mary, so that they would comfort one another in his departure".[230] This is a clear example that

---

[226] John 7:5, (NIV).

[227] Hebrews 11:35.

[228] B. H. Carroll. *Bible Commentary: The Four Gospels. Volume 6. Volume II.* Trd. Sara A. Hale. (Terrassa (Barcelona), Spain. Editorial CLIE. 1986), 50-51

[229] John 19:25-26, (NIV).

[230] William Barclay. *Commentary on the New Testament: Volume 6: JOHN: II.* (Terrassa (Barcelona), Spain. Editorial CLIE. 1996), 291

even if everyone abandons you and you don't have a safe place, the goodness and care of Jesus Christ will never leave you without a place where you can be safe and comforted at the same time.

The truth is that, although the Gospel of Jesus Christ provokes conjecture, the one who was crucified and now resurrected, still cares for you! This means, the Gospel of Jesus Christ, being the Word of God, is comfort to the human being who has been forsaken and discarded by humans.

Jesus' words: *There you have your mother*, are still a refuge for all who have been forsaken and rejected in this world.

III.- A PLACE FOR THE HOMELESS.

When I gave myself to Jesus Christ to be saved and minister in His Kingdom, I told my mother and she told me that this work was for homosexuals. A short time later I told my father that I would work in the Work of Jesus Christ as his missionary or as a pastor. His answer was blunt. He told me that I would never be a pastor, that it wasn't for me. In my insistence on preparing to serve the Lord, my father said to me, "If that is what you want to do, do it, but don't count on me. From now on you have no father".[231]

Heartbroken I left my father's house. He was a Christian and was sure he would be glad that his eldest son was a servant of Jesus Christ. My thoughts and emotions failed me. However, I took strength and comfort in the Scripture that says, "Even though my father and mother abandon me, you,

---

[231] *I spoke with my Father*, Mr. Alejandro Barajas, at his home in Lombardy Michoacán in the summer of 1968.

Lord, will take care of me".[232] And, to this day, fifty-three years later, God has taken care of me.

The gospel of Jesus Christ is good news for those in the world and family members that have rejected it. It is the Gospel that tell us that Jesus gives us protection and care. It is the Gospel that puts us in the Church, which becomes Our Family in faith.

Jesus Christ had said that He would establish the Church: "... I'm going to build my church; and not even the power of death can overcome it",[233] were his prophetic words. And, in that place called Mount Calvary or the place of the Skull, in the midst of that painful scenario, Jesus reaffirms his purpose of building his Church and proclaims it as a fact when he told his followers: "... when the Holy Spirit comes upon you, you will receive power and go out to bear witness to me, in Jerusalem, throughout the region of Judea and Samaria, and even in the farthest parts of the earth".[234]

Days later it is inaugurated within the city of Jerusalem with admirable phenomena: *Tongues of fire, a strong wind, an earth tremor and a compression of language.* The Bible says that: "On the day of Pentecost, all believers were gathered in one place. Suddenly, a noise was heard from the sky resembling the roar of a strong, impetuous wind that filled the house where they were sitting. Then, something resembling flames or tongues of fire appeared and landed on each of them. And all those present were filled with the Holy Spirit and began to speak in other languages, as the Holy Spirit gave them that ability".[235]

---

[232]   Psalm 27;10, (DHH).
[233]   Matthew 16:18b, (DHH).
[234]   Acts of the Apostles 1:8, (DHH).
[235]   Acts of the Apostles 2:1-4, (NLT).

This is the Family of the Homeless; It is the Church with which, from that moment on the Calvary, until today, it comforts and protects. Jesus' words, when he said, "There you have your mother," remain comforting because, like Mary, the mother of Jesus of Nazareth, she obtained a place and a person for her protection. As a Christian person you must be convinced that by believing in Jesus Christ he not only has comfort and shelter in Him but has also been received into the Family of God.

CONCLUSION.

The words of Jesus: *There you have your mother,* who by tradition has been called; The Careful Word still has a connotation of blessing for every son and daughter of God. That is, if you are a Christian and you seize the courage and love that God has placed in your life to face all kinds of situations adverse to your beliefs and practices, God will take care of you!

Woman, there you have your son, and —*There you have your mother,* are expressions of the Crucified One who affirm that: "Until the very end of his life – Jesus – was thinking more of the pains of others than of his own".[236]

Brother, sister in Christ Jesus, the Lord will always seek the best for you. He will always have a comforting word for your life. He is the God of all consolation!

---

[236]   William Barclay. *Commentary on the New Testament: Volume 6: JOHN: II.* (Terrassa (Barcelona), Spain. Editorial CLIE. 1996), 291.

MUTED MOUTHS

"From noon to mid-afternoon, the whole
earth was left in darkness".
Matthew 27:45, (NIV).

INTRODUCTION.

The beatings and whippings they gave to Jesus Christ were terrible; it was a physical pain that he endured from beginning to end. Now, as I said in the previous message, as if the pain of being there crucified was not enough, he still had to suffer the emotional or psychological pain provided by the soldiers, the religious leaders and some of the Jews present in the *Place of the Skull*; it must have been very emotional pain!

It seems that all he suffered should have been enough. However, he still had much more terrible pain than physical and emotional; Before he died, he felt terrible pain, which I call: Family Pain. What was that pain like? I invite you to examine it briefly with the following three points; These three points are another part of this terrible pain that Jesus experienced in the *Place of the Skull*.

Why did he call it: Family Pain? Because it is a spiritual abandonment on the part of the Father God. The Father did not want to see the disfigured face of Jesus; he was not only disfigured by the blows he had received, but much more by the sin of all humanity he was carrying upon himself.

What did the Father do to hide the face of His Beloved Son? He provoked a natural phenomenon; it caused a miracle at a time that according to science was almost impossible to happen. And yet, the Bible says, "From noon to mid-afternoon, the whole earth was left in darkness".[237] Darkness at the sunniest hour! Well, what do we learn from that darkness?

I.- WHAT HAPPENED?

Yes, to find the lessons of this incident, we must ask ourselves: What happened there on the Calvary? Let us remember that: "From nine o'clock in the morning until noon the Calvary had been a place of great activity. The soldiers had performed their various tasks, the passers-by had blasphemed. Chief priests, scribes, and elders had mocked Jesus Christ. The thieves had insulted him, although one of them repented. Jesus had already spoken his first three words. Then, at twelve o'clock in the day, something of a very dramatic character happens. Suddenly the earth darkens".[238]

The fact that the Evangelist Matthew mentions it implies that this darkness was nothing normal, it was a somewhat capricious darkness. Apparently, it was an intense darkness and was recorded in scripture as a fact that must be remembered in

---

[237]   Matthew 27:45, (NIV).
[238]   William Hendriksen. *The Gospel of Matthew: Commentary on the New Testament.* (Grand Rapids, Michigan. Distributed by T.E.L.L. Subcommittee on Christian Literature. 1986),1017

the course of history. It was a darkness that "occurred when it was least expected, at noon, and lasted three hours".[239] Yes, it was a somewhat capricious darkness! In this divine action, more than capricious, as I call it, the mouths became silent. Everyone present on the Calvary was silent! If anything could be heard, it was laments of horror and despair. If anything was heard, it was questions like: What's going on? Why this darkness? What are we doing? Is this a punishment from God?

Well, what was happening? What we know from the Scripture is that: "The mocking tone of the witnesses on the Calvary suddenly becomes gloomy".[240] All mouths are silent! If anything, they utter anything, it is expressions of amazement at what they are experiencing. But everyone present on the Calvary was silent!

Some think that the cause of the darkness was the consequence of a solar eclipse.[241] If it was an eclipse of the sun, then, we can rightly say that: This amazing eclipse was intended to cover the mouths of the blasphemers who mocked Christ while he was on the lookout for the cross".[242]

A solar eclipse!? A somewhat good theory. However, it seems to us that: "It was not a solar eclipse, because Easter took place on a full moon; rather it was an unusual act of God".[243] That is, when we talk about the darkness that

---

[239] William Hendriksen. *The Gospel of Matthew: Commentary on the New Testament.* (Grand Rapids, Michigan. Distributed by T.E.L.L. Subcommittee on Christian Literature. 1986),1017

[240] Matthew Henry. *Exegetical-Devotional Commentary on the Entire Bible: Matthew.* Td. Francisco Lacueva. (Terrassa (Barcelona), Spain. Editorial CLIE. 1984), 548

[241] Matthew Henry. *Comentario Exegético-Devocional a toda la Biblia: Mateo.* Td. Francisco Lacueva. (Terrassa (Barcelona), España. Editorial CLIE. 1984), 548.

[242] Michael J. Wilkins. *Bible Commentary with Application: MATTHEW: From the Biblical Text to a Contemporary Application.* (Nashville, Tennessee, USA. Editorial Vida. 2016), 902.

[243] Michael J. Wilkins. *Bible Commentary with Application: MATTHEW: From the Biblical Text to a Contemporary Application.* (Nashville, Tennessee, USA. Editorial Vida. 2016), 902.

happened on the Calvary from twelve o'clock in the day until three o'clock in the afternoon, this darkness "cannot refer to an eclipse in the technical or astronomical sense... for that was impossible at the time of Easter... Moreover, such an eclipse could not have lasted three hours".[244] And, less with a density like that suggested in the reading of the Gospel of Matthew, because it does not say that the place was clouded but says that: All the earth was left in darkness.[245]

So, it was not a solar eclipse, but it was a miracle that silenced the mouths of those present on the Calvary. Apparently, even the mouth of the Lord Jesus Himself was silent for three hours.

It was a sepulchral silence. Everyone was silent! The forces of death were present, the Son of God was in the last moments of his human and divine agony: Human because Jesus was and is a true human being, born of a woman named Mary and, divine, because he was carrying on his divinity; on his person, the weight of sin of each one of us.

For my liking, it would have been much better for each of those present at the *Place of the Skull*, witnessing this marvelous miracle, to change their hearts for the better. However: "Even when their hearts were not changed, at least their mouths were muted, perplexed by what was happening".[246]

One day, unlike the Calvary, every mouth will open. It will open to lament or to give a cry of Hallelujah! Christ reigns! That day will be when the Crucified, Dead and Risen, appears in the clouds, at His Second Coming. On that day,

---

[244]   William Hendriksen. The Gospel of Matthew: Commentary on the New Testament. (Grand Rapids, Michigan. Distributed by T.E.L.L. Subcommittee on Christian Literature. 1986),1017

[245]   Matthew 27:45, (NIV).

[246]   Matthew Henry. *Exegetical-Devotional Commentary on the Entire Bible: Matthew.* Td. Francisco Lacueva. (Terrassa (Barcelona), Spain. Editorial CLIE. 1984), 548.

every mouth will be opened! It will be a completely different event than what happened on the Calvary: An event full of light! The glory of Jesus Christ will illuminate the whole earth! Darkness, for many, will disappear! That is, that day will be a glorious day

II.- THE DARKNESS, IN THE BIBLICAL USE.

"Much has been written about this darkness. What caused it? How much territory did it cover? Did it have any meaning? ... What we can say is that 'God produced it'."[247] And yes, it does have a meaning, a meaning that we will see later, because here we will focus on the biblical use of darkness.

From our own experience we know that light and darkness are antagonistic; they don't get along with each other. We also know that light is a symbol of good while darkness is of evil. Now, in both the Old and New Testaments, light symbolizes God, while darkness suggests the opposite of Him.

Obscurity or darkness in the Bible means:

1.- The wicked.
"Discretion will keep you; It will preserve your intelligence, to get rid of the evil way, of the men who speak perversities, who leave the right paths, to walk on dark paths; who rejoice in doing evil, who strike in the perversities of vice". (Prov. 2:13-14, NVI).

---

[247] William Hendriksen. *The Gospel of Matthew: Commentary on the New Testament.* (Grand Rapids, Michigan. Distributed by T.E.L.L. Subcommittee On Christian Literature. 1986),1017

2.- *The trial.*

"The Lord said to Moses, 'Lift up your arms to heaven, that all Egypt may be covered with darkness, darkness so dense that it can be felt!'." (Exodus 10:21, NVI).

"And to that useless servant throw him outside, into the darkness, where there will be weeping and gnashing of teeth". (Matthew 25:30, NLT).

3.- *Death.*

"In the shadows of death, where everything is forgotten, will there be anyone who recognizes your righteousness and wonders?" (Psalm 88:13, DHH).

If we summarize what I have said above, we will notice that: "Salvation brings light to those who are in darkness (Matt. 4:16). The moment of God's supreme judgment, the day of the Lord, is a day of darkness (Am 5:18, 20; Jl 2:22; Soph 1:15; Mt 24:29; Revelation 6:12-17)".[248] It will be another day or time when the mouths will be muted again.

Throughout the earthly ministry of Jesus Christ, He always had a struggle against the hosts of evil, those that symbolized darkness and the existence of sin. That is, in the Gospels we notice Christ in his conflict with darkness. His culmination of the struggle was on the Calvary; there, the victory, was total and definitive.

---

[248] William Hendriksen. *The Gospel of Matthew: Commentary on the New Testament.* (Grand Rapids, Michigan. Distributed by T.E.L.L. Subcommittee On Christian Literature. 1986),1017.

In a symbolic way, what happened to that darkness on the Calvary? What else does this divine miracle performed in the *Place of the Skull"* teach us? That darkness manifested:

1.- That Satan has limitations. Even with all the effort he made to defeat Jesus Christ, he finally realizes that he cannot overcome the Crucified One. He realizes that even without his Father's support, the power of Jesus Christ is far greater than his. Satan came there and there he stopped; he could not advance any further. As much as He incited the people, Jesus Christ continued to love them and at one point, Said, "Father, forgive them because they don't know what they do".[249] That is, Jesus Christ begged the Father for forgiveness for those who insulted him, saying to Him: Father, forgive them, they do not realize that Satan is inciting them against me. Forgive them.

Satanic power was limited! When Jesus was arrested, He surrendered voluntarily and clarified to them: "... this is your hour, and the power of darkness".[250] It is, then, "a passing victory of the forces of evil (I Co 2:8); the final victory belongs to God (Jn. 1:5; Col 1:13)".[251] That satanic power that was inciting people to insult Jesus, that satanic power that incited religious people to blaspheme against Jesus Christ, from one moment to the next, all mouths went silent! The satanic power couldn't go any further! Even Satan himself, it seems, also became silent. The crucified one limited his power!

2.- The darkness manifested that God was disgusted with humanity for having crucified his Beloved Son. And since his Beloved Son had voluntarily given himself to the Redemptive Work, then, God the Father, did not want to see, nor did he

---

[249]   Luke 23:34, (KJV, 1960).

[250]   Luke 22:53c, (KJV, 1960)

[251]   Commentary on *the Schematic Study Bible*. (Brazil. United Bible Societies. 2010), 1549.

want the people to continue to see the disfigured face of his Son because of the blows and the weight of sin, so he covered it with the same symbol of sin: With darkness! At the same time, he silenced the mouths of those present on the Calvary.

3.- The darkness of the Calvary symbolizes "the divine judgment on the sins of the world".[252]

The Bible says that the wage of sin is death and then adds that it is established for mankind to die only once and then judgment comes. The darkness illustrates that there will come a day when some will go through critical moments; it will be a time when their mouths will be closed because they will have no valid argument against the King of kings and Lord of lords.

However, amid that chaos of darkness, there will be people who, because of the love of God manifested in His Son Jesus Christ and His Redeemer forgiveness, won in those three hours of darkness, will enjoy the victory of Jesus and will be with Him in His glory. There, the mouths will be opened again, but now to say, "The Lamb who was sacrificed is worthy to receive power and wealth, wisdom and strength, honor, glory and praise!".[253] Amen!

III.- DARKNESS SYMBOLIZES A DIVINE REJECTION.

Although I have already mentioned it, I repeat it again: "That darkness is the beginning of God's judgment on a world

---

[252]   Michael J. Wilkins. *Bible Commentary with Application: MATTHEW: From the Biblical Text to a Contemporary Application.* (Nashville, Tennessee, USA. Editorial Vida. 2016), 902.

[253]   Revelation 5:12, (DHH)"

that condemned to death the one who brought the kingdom of God".[254] It is true that Jesus Christ showed the great love He has for every human being; I have no doubt about that. However, the other side of the coin is that everyone, did you hear me right? Everyone! The entire human race will go through a judgment; it is the judgment in which the supreme Judge will make the following statement: "When the Son of man comes, surrounded by splendor and all his angels, he will sit on his glorious throne. And the King will say to those on his right: 'Come you, those who have been blessed by my Father; receive the kingdom that is prepared for you since God made the world'. Then the King will say to those on his left: 'Depart from me, those who deserved condemnation; go into the eternal fire prepared for the devil and his angels'."[255]

Harsh words! Yes, they are tough! But not as harsh as the rejection that Jesus Christ suffered from His Father when He was bearing your sin and mine. Both cases are incomprehensible, but at the same time true.

It was at that time of divine rejection that the earth darkened. "But what was it that darkened it?".[256] I think the best answer is that, Jesus, burdened with the sin of all humanity, the sin of all human history, God the Father, who is All Holy, did not want to see his Son in those conditions and covered him with a cloak of darkness; a rejection that Jesus felt deeply: It was the rejection of His Father! Jesus had obeyed him in everything; he always did the Father's will, and now, at the time when he most needed his support, he abandoned him! And, Jesus, felt the family rejection.

---

[254]   Commentary on the *Schematic Study Bible*. (Brazil. United Bible Societies. 2010), 1480

[255]   Matthew 25:31-45, (DHH).

[256]   William Hendriksen. *The Gospel of Matthew: Commentary on the New Testament*. (Grand Rapids, Michigan. Distributed by T.E.L.L. Subcommittee On Christian Literature. 1986),1017

This, then, was to be expected, for the Bible says that Jesus was completely saturated with sin, though he did not commit any sin in all his earthly life. However, the apostle Paul said that: "... Christ has rescued us from the curse dictated in the law. When he was hung on the cross, he carried upon himself the curse of our misdeeds. For it is written, 'Cursed is everyone who is hung on some wood'."[257] The 1960 King James Version says: *Christ redeemed us from the curse of the law, made by us a curse (for it is written: Cursed is everyone who is hung on a tree).*

Not an easy Act of Redeeming. On the contrary, it was an act of courage, it was a supreme decision, it was a step of great pain. "It is suggested – in the text we have read – that at that moment the whole weight of the sin of the world fell upon the heart and being of Jesus; that this was the time when the One who knew no sin was made sin for us (2 Corinthians 5:21); and that the punishment He suffered for us implied the inevitable separation from God".[258] This is what produces sin: Separation from God! That is, as long as you and I remain in sin, we are separated from God.

So, what we must consider in this case is that what happened there, on the Calvary, "was a miracle, a special act of God",[259] which silenced the mouths of those present and that leaves us a path to freedom. He set us free!

---

[257] Galatians 3:13, (NLT).

[258] William Barclay. *Commentary on the New Testament: Volume 2: MATTHEW: II.* Trd. Alberto Araujo. (Terrassa (Barcelona), Spain. Editorial CLIE. 1997), 425.

[259] William Hendriksen. *The Gospel of Matthew: Commentary on the New Testament.* (Grand Rapids, Michigan. Distributed by T.E.L.L. Subcommittee On Christian Literature. 1986),1017

CONCLUSION.

The darkness closed the mouths of all who were in the *Place of the Skull*. No matter what the mockers, the abusive soldiers, the blasphemers, the thieves, and the religious say, one day, God will shut their mouths to them.

My question to you is: Will your mouth also close? Could it be that on that day you will have no excuse before the one who was crucified and who is now in glory?

You and I will stand one day before him who was crucified, who died, and who rose again; One day we will stand before the Lord Jesus Christ! On that day, will your mouth be opened to worship the one who lives and reigns forever? Or, will it open up to utter laments? What will you say on that day? Today you have the opportunity to know what will come out of your mouth.

WHY, LORD?

-The fourth word: The word pathetic-
"About three in the afternoon Jesus cried out in a
loud voice, 'Eli, Eli, lema sabachthani?' (which means
'My God, my God, why have you forsaken me?')".
Matthew 27:46, (NIV).

INTRODUCTION.

Traditionally, this fourth word of Jesus, spoken from the cross, is called: The Pathetic Word. *Pathetic is*: which denotes great anguish or moral suffering; That is, we have reached the deepest point of the cross. Jesus felt helpless by the Father. By the way, we have come to the most mysterious text of this whole scene of the Passion of Christ.

To continue with the question of our theme: Why, Lord? we ask ourselves, saying: Why is the text of Matthew 27:46 the most mysterious of the scene of the Passion? And in response we ask ourselves three other questions: How is it possible that God has abandoned the righteous? How is it possible that the father abandoned the Beloved Son in whom his complacency was? How is it possible for God to forsake Himself?

I don't have the right answers to these questions, but what I do have are three other questions:

I.- WHY DID JESUS HAVE TO GO THROUGH ABANDONMENT?

The Evangelist Matthew relates that: "About three in the afternoon Jesus cried out in a loud voice, 'Eli, Eli, *lema sabachthani?*' (Which means 'My God, my God, why have you forsaken me?')".[260] "Jesus' expressions and his painful cries on the cross are the consequence of his human suffering. ... None of these cries are as powerful as, *'My God, my God, why have you forsaken me?'* (27:45-46)".[261]

> It is a cry in which Jesus was expressing the pain of experiencing in full awareness the consequences of the wages of sin, which was death and at the same time separation from the One who is All Holy.
>
> Jesus was "experiencing death for the sins of mankind".[262]
>
> It is, therefore, "A saying – in a loud voice – before which we must bow down

---

[260] Matthew 27: 46a, (NIV).

[261] Michael J Wilkins. *Bible Commentary with Application: MATTHEW: From the Biblical Text to a Contemporary Application.* (Nashville, Tennessee, USA. Editorial Vida. 2016), 918.

[262] Michael J Wilkins. *Bible Commentary with Application: MATTHEW: From the Biblical Text to a Contemporary Application.* (Nashville, Tennessee, USA. Editorial Vida. 2016), 918.

ourselves with reverence, although we must also try to understand it".[263]

I invite you to notice the tone in which Jesus expressed these words:

*It is not a lament or cry of resignation. Jesus suffered martyrdom, but He was not a martyr; he did everything voluntarily.

*It was not a lament of resentment because His Father had abandoned him. Jesus knew He was bearing sin and that affected His fellowship with the Father.

*It is not a cry of one who does not understand what is happening. Jesus knew that this was the only way to redeem man from the bondage of sin.

* It is not a cry in an interrogative way with contempt, but in a sentimental way; Jesus feels the abandonment of his Father.

It is, therefore, a cry of someone who is aware of what he is doing and, although he is abandoned by his Father, he continues with his Redemptive Mission.

Certainly, the abandonment of his Father is painful for the Crucified One. That is why he expresses it with a great voice; it was a cry of:

*I need your support! My god! My god!
*It was an interrogation of deep family grief!
The Father abandoned him.

263 William, Barclay. *Comentario al Nuevo Testamento: Volumen 2: MATEO: II*. Trd. Alberto Araujo. (Terrassa (Barcelona), España. Editorial CLIE. 1997), 424.

* It was a cry that "indicates the extreme intensity of his pain and anguish. The full weight of sin was upon Him.

* It was a cry that came out of - the force that remained in his human nature.

* It was a cry that indicated – "the longing of his spirit to express it".[264] *My God, my God, why have you forsaken me?* A question that shows the longing for his father's companionship in those critical moments.

In the interrogation of the Crucified One there is a double expression: *My God, my God.* This is, even in the most frightening, disastrous, and painful circumstances that Christ was going through, even God was their God! A perfect example that in whatever circumstance you find yourself in, God will always be your God!

Another of the great truths that we find in Christian Theology is that at that moment when darkness covered the face of Jesus Christ the face of God the Father was also hidden from the presence of Jesus who bore your sin and mine. That is to say: "The father's face was taken away from his Son so that all of us who deserve to be outside his holiness, outside the presence of the almighty God, may now live in his presence".[265]

[264]   Matthew Henry. *Exegetical-Devotional Commentary on the Entire Bible: Matthew.* Td. Francisco Lacueva. (Terrassa (Barcelona), Spain. Editorial CLIE. 1984), 549.

[265]   Aaron Burgner. *Commentary on The Gospel.* (La Habra, California. Internet. Published by the Indigenous Educational Center. Retrieved August 26, 2021), ¿? https://www.facebook.com/centroeducativoindigena/photos/a.571382076259692/3385425331522005/

II.- WHY DID JESUS IDENTIFY WITH THE LOST HUMAN BEING?

This is the second question on this morning. Why did Jesus identify with the lost human being? Incredibly, the All Holy, the one who never committed a single sin:

Jesus Christ had the courage and humility to identify with the poor. Jesus, in his earthly life, never identified with the powerful of his time. Jesus was born humble, in an almost unknown village on the territory of Galilee. Jesus was not born in the popular city of Jerusalem where almost all the kings of Judah were born.

He had the audacity to identify with the sinful person. He touched lepers who were cursed or sinners for being lepers. He ate in the homes of the publicans who were considered sinners. He let a woman considered a sinner touch his feet.

He had the kindness to identify with the person who is separated from God. His goal was and is to unite people separated by sin with the All-Holy God.

Jesus had the courage to identify with the one who knows that he is unable to attain salvation. He made himself the bridge so that the sinner could reach God. He said that it was the Way, the truth, and the life and that no one could reach the Father except through him.[266]

*With good reason, the apostle Paul said that Jesus became cursed; no one did it for him, he willingly identified with the race cursed by sin.[267] In the moments when Satan tempted him by offering him the kingdoms of this world, Jesus Christ made the decision to continue ministering for another kingdom: For the kingdom of God! When the Enemy

---

[266] John 14:6. Transliterated by Eleazar Barajas.
[267] Galatians 3:13.

offered him riches, He said no. When He offered power, He said no. Even when He offered to throw Himself into the void because the angels would hold Him, His answer was no.[268]

Jesus knew what awaited Him: The Cross. He knew that, by identifying with each of the human conditions, it would draw him closer to the Cross, and yet he did so out of love for humanity! When he reached the cross, his face was too disfigured somewhat by the blows the soldiers had given him and by the weight of sin that was upon him. The prophet Isaiah wondered, "Who has believed our message and to whom has the power of the Lord been revealed?" And then he comments on God's Messiah, saying, "He grew in his presence as a tender offspring, as a root of dry earth. There was no beauty or majesty in him; his appearance was not attractive and nothing in his appearance made him desirable. Despised and rejected by men, a man of sorrows, made for suffering. Everyone avoided looking at him; he was despised, and they didn't appreciate him".[269] This is the scene that could be seen on the Calvary. Jesus was completely disfigured and, moreover, bearing the sin of all. Rightly so His Father, in his heartache at what they were doing and saying to His Beloved Son, decided to hide His face from the unlookers and at the same time from His holiness. And so, with good reason, Jesus, feeling the separation from his Father, exclaims, *"My God, my God, why have you forsaken me?"*[270]

In these conditions, the Father, who is also All Holy, in the most agonizing hours of the crucified, could not have a communion with his Beloved Son! And, Jesus Christ, in the most critical hours there on the Calvary, felt the abandonment

---

[268]   Matthew 4:1-11
[269]   Isaiah 53:1-4, (NIV).
[270]   Matthew 27:46, (KJV, 1960).

of his Father. And that's why he cries out, *"My God, my God, why have you forsaken me?"*[271]

In this sense, the cry of Jesus on the cross is intended to point out the deep abyss that exists between God and the human being. By crying out in the state of helplessness, Jesus reveals that, in the deepest sense of the word, all of us are helpless; while we notice that all of us need the shelter from which he can save us.

In this expression of Jesus, "we have what must have been the most mind-boggling phrase in all of evangelical history: The cry of Jesus: 'My God, my God, why have you forsaken me?'."[272] This is a cry that is still heard in the world announcing, like a trumpet, that the Redemption of humanity had begun. The Righteous One was forsaken so that we would be protected!

Why did Jesus identify with the lost human being? Because his Mission was a Redemptive Mission. The only way to fulfill this mission was to identify one hundred percent with humanity, that is why he was born like any other human being; he lived as all human beings of his time lived, with the exception that he never sinned. And he suffered all the pains, and much more than any human being has ever suffered.

So, returning to Christian theology, with it we have been taught that sin is separation and death. The cry of the Crucified One was because he was experiencing family separation; His father had forsaken Him because of the sin that was upon Him, and he was in the last minutes of earthly life. I can therefore say that your sin and mine separated him from God and caused him physical death. Jesus died, not only to give us freedom from our sins, but also to give us eternal life.

Jesus identified with us!

---

[271]   Matthew 27:46, (NIV).
[272]   William, Barclay. *Commentary on the New Testament: Volume 2: MATTHEW: II.* Trd. Alberto Araujo. (Terrassa (Barcelona), Spain. Editorial CLIE. 1997), 424.

III.- WHY DID PEOPLE GET ANGRY AGAINST JESUS?

We come to the third question of Why. Why did people become angry against Jesus? The Father's abandonment was: "The gravest of all Christ's sufferings, and that is why it was here that he uttered his most painful complaint. Until then, the Father had been close to Him; now he moves away from it, not physically, but morally. ... there is nothing that causes as much pain as physical closeness without comfort, without help and without support".[273] And Christ Jesus went through this bitter and desperate experience.

Evangelist Matthew says that when the soldiers heard Jesus' plea, they thought he was calling the prophet Elijah. However, some, or perhaps one of them, set out to comfort the thirsty Crucified One a little; he offered him vinegar. "Others, on the contrary, continued with their purpose of mocking him..."[274] They said to the merciful soldier, "...Leave him, let us see if Elijah comes to save him".[275]

Clearly, the expression *leave* or *leave him*, indicates, "do not give him any help or comfort; let him manage it with Elijah".[276]

It is because of hearts so hard and cruel, full of sin, that Jesus Christ came to the cross. It is for this kind of person that the Lord Jesus had to cry out from the depths of his being with a great cry of anguish: " 'Eli, Eli, *sabactani motto*?', which means 'My God, my God, why have you forsaken

[273]   Matthew Henry. *Exegetical-Devotional Commentary on the Entire Bible: Matthew.* Td. Francisco Lacueva. (Terrassa (Barcelona), Spain. Editorial CLIE. 1984), 549.

[274]   Matthew Henry. *Comentario Exegético-Devocional a toda la Biblia: Mateo.* Td. Francisco Lacueva. (Terrassa (Barcelona), España. Editorial CLIE. 1984), 550.

[275]   Matthew 27:49, (DHH).

[276]   Matthew Henry. *Exegetical-Devotional Commentary on the Entire Bible: Matthew.* Td. Francisco Lacueva. (Terrassa (Barcelona), Spain. Editorial CLIE. 1984), 550.

me?'"[277] Jesus Christ used the expression found in Psalm 22, a Psalm "written by a sick, dying man who is also persecuted by cruel enemies".[278] What the psalmist expresses in his first verse is an expression of pain and despair, matters that apply very aptly to Jesus' sufferings on the cross of the Calvary.[279]

"Psalm 22 arose from an experience of very intense suffering. The one who suffers feels very lonely, abandoned, but he continues to trust in God".[280] so he cries out with deep feeling: "'*Eli, Eli, sabactani motto?*', which means 'My God, my God, why have you forsaken me?'

The longing of Jesus Christ with His Redemptive and Saving Work is to make a new world; a world where God's justice, love, kindness, and mercy are the queens among the human race. A world where the Fruit of the Spirit shines with a light like the most powerful lamps we know. A light that can be seen at great distances like the lights that exist in the new World Trade Center, where the Twin Towers of New York were.

This kind of new world would be ideal for the One who one day, back on the Calvary, exclaimed, *My God, my God, why have you forsaken me*? "However, the present world of evil has not come to an end, nor is the new one still present in its full and definitive form. Evil and sin continue to exist".[281] This is a present reality, very much of us.

---

[277] Matthew 27:46, (NLT).

[278] Commentary on *the Schematic Study Bible*. (Brazil. United Bible Societies. 2010), 795.

[279] Commentary on *the Schematic Study Bible*. (Brazil. United Bible Societies. 2010), 795.

[280] Eduardo Nelson G., Mervin Breneman, Ricardo Souto Copeiro and others. *Hispanic World Bible Commentary: Psalms: Volume 8*. (El Paso, Texas. Editorial Mundo Hispano. 2002), 119.

[281] Douglas J. Moo. Romans: *Commentary with application; from the biblical text to a contemporary application*. (Miami, Florida. Editorial Vida. 2011), 206.

CONCLUSION.

Why do things or events happen in our life that we don't understand? We don't always have an answer to why, and so, like Jesus, we must say It shall be done. Our plea must be my God, my God, your will be done.

TRUE HUMAN BEING

-The fifth word: The expressive word- "I am thirsty".

"After this, since Jesus knew that everything
had already been fulfilled, and that the Scripture
would be fulfilled, he said: - 'I am thirsty'."
John 19:28, (DHH).

INTRODUCTION.

Have you ever felt a thirst to such an extent that you feel that
your tongue sticks to your palate? Have you ever felt a thirst
to such an extent that you can no longer speak? Have you
ever felt such an intense thirst that you would be willing to
drink any kind of water? If your answers are yes, it is because
you are a human being, if you were a robot or a ghost or an
inanimate thing, the lack of water would not affect you.

Now think about this. Jesus was arrested Thursday night,
from The Last Week of His Earthly Life, he was not allowed
to sleep all night. At nine o'clock on Friday morning, he was
crucified. Suppose he was arrested at 12:00 p.m. on Thursday,
he walked to the house of the high priests, he walked to the

palace of Pontius Pilate, he walked to the residence of Herod, he returned to the Palace of Pilate, he walked to the top of Mount Calvary and, moreover, he already had more than three hours on the cross and with the incandescent sun of Jerusalem, it was logical that Jesus would be thirsty.[282]

What we can see in the historical account presented to us by the Evangelists about this terrible scene is admirable and at the same time miraculous; How could Jesus endure so long without drinking water? Remember that he was bleeding and that requires more water to avoid dehydration. How could he still scream when the lack of water dries his mouth? There are at least three lessons about this scene and this expression of the Crucified One that we must meditate on this morning:

During the course of the story about the life of Jesus Christ, enough stories, tales, myths, legends, different philosophies regarding the life and ministry of Jesus Christ, and theological concepts have emerged. For example: "Docetism (from the Greek koine δοκεῖν/δόκησις, dokeîn 'to appear, to appear', dokēsis 'apparition, ghost'), in the history of Christianity, designates a set of heterodox Christological tendencies present in the first centuries of Christianity about the true nature of Jesus Christ, his historical and bodily existence, and above all his human form, which was a simple appearance without any carnal nature. In general, it is taken as the belief that the sufferings and humanity of Jesus Christ were apparent and not real, his human form was a mere illusion".[283]

---

[282] AccuWeather. For example, according to this institution, on April 2, which was Friday, of this year 2021, the maximum temperature in Jerusalem was 53 ° and the minimum of 45 °. Today, August 31, 2021, the temperature in Jerusalem is 74°F. (La Habra, California. Internet. Retrieved August 31, 2021), ¿? https://www.accuweather.com/es/il/jerusalem/213225/april-weather/213225?year=2021

[283] Wikipedia, the free encyclopedia. *Docetism*. (La Habra, California. Internet. Retrieved September 7, 2021), ¿? https://es.wikipedia.org/wiki/Docetismo

One of the first-century philosophies of the Christian Era is Gnosticism. In my book entitled: And We Saw His Glory, I have commented that: "Gnosticism (from ancient Greek: γνωστικός gnōstikós, 'to have knowledge') is a set of ancient ideas and religious systems that originated in the first century between Jewish and ancient Christian sects".[284]

Two of his main doctrines were: First, the separation of the god of creation from the god of redemption. The second, its emphasis on secret knowledge that only divine persons could understand.[285]

This philosophy, from that time until today, have spoken of Jesus Christ in different ways, some of them have even stripped him of his divinity, leaving Jesus as a mere man.

For example, the Austrian philosopher, literary scholar, educator, artist, playwright, social thinker and occultist, Rudolf Steiner, taught that: "The process of maturation of Jesus, which occurred in his 30s ... attained the state of Christ".[286] That is to say that before he was only a mere man, he was not God; It was just Jesus of Nazareth. Theologian John Hepp, one of my professors at the Biblical Institute and Seminary of Puebla, Puebla, Mexico, believed the same!

Yes, Jesus Christ was a true human being! The Bible assures it. He was born like any other human being, his mother was Mary, a young woman from Nazareth in Galilee.[287]Because

---

[284]   Wikipedia: the free encyclopedia. *Gnosticism*. (La Habra, California. Internet. Retrieved August 28, 2021), ¿? https://es.wikipedia.org/wiki/Gnosticismo

[285]   Leticia Calcada: General Editor. *Gnosticism*. Holman Illustrated Bible Dictionary. (Nashville, Tennessee. USED. B&H Publishing Group. 2008), 694.

[286]   Luis Alberto Hará. - *A mystical look at the Figure of Jesus Christ* (or the archetypal divinity of the human being). (La Habra, California. Internet. Article published on December 25, 2015. Retrieved August 27, 2021), ¿? https://pijamasurf.com/2015/12/una-mirada-mistica-a-la-figura-de-cristo-o-la-divinidad-arquetipica-al-interior-del-ser-humano/

[287]   Luke 1:26-31.

of a royal edict, Jesus was born in Bethlehem of Judea.[288]That is, Jesus was born among the Jews and grew up in the village of Nazareth so that the Scripture that he would be called Nazarene would be fulfilled.[289]

Jesus Christ suffered everything that human beings suffer pain, hunger, cold, heat, thirst, anguish, tired of walking, fell asleep in a boat and even became angry.[290]

Yes, Jesus was a human being with the same needs that all human beings have!

Now, this does not take away from the one who also WAS and IS God. The god of redemption, with lower case, of which Gnostic philosophy speaks, although HE WAS and IS a person, he also IS God, with a capital letter: He is the God of Redemption, also with a capital letter! The author of the book to the Hebrews says about Jesus Christ: "For our High Priest may commiserate with our weakness, for he too was subjected to the same trials as we are; only he never sinned".[291]

Thus, "in order to 'come to be merciful and faithful High Priest', the Son of God– that is, Jesus – 'must be in all things like his brethren'; and that he 'is mighty to succor those who are tempted' because 'he himself suffered being tempted' (2:17s)".[292] This means that Christians have in heaven a person who is extremely powerful; that he is a human being but at the same time he is eternal God and that he is with an

---

[288]   Luke 2:1-7

[289]   Matthew 2:23

[290]   "... all my bones are dislocated. My heart has become like wax, and it melts in my bowels" (Ps. 22:14, NVI); Mark 11:12; John 4:6-8; "Jesus, meanwhile, was at the stern, sleeping on a head (Mark 4:38, NVI); " And making a scourge of ropes, he cast everyone out of the temple, with the sheep and the oxen; he scattered the coins of the money changers and overturned the tables" (John 2:15). "

[291]   Hebrews 4:15, (DHH).

[292]   F. F. Bruce. *The Epistle to the Hebrews.* (Grand Rapids, Michigan. New Creation and William B. Eerdmans Publishing Company. 1987), 86.

unparalleled capacity, in such a way that he can be by our side in all conflicts and despairs because, He Himself experienced these sufferings.[293]

Having gone through human experiences, then: "The glorious High Priest is also admirable for being compassionate. Being God he is, by divine nature, distant from men, above all from their imperfections and limitations, but, as he is also a perfect man, he is absolutely close, so much so that one of the Trinity has become a companion of limitations and sufferings of men".[294] That *"one"* is called Jesus of Nazareth; the man/God who has become the intermediary between the All Holy God and the imperfect and sinful human being. He was a human being just like us without leaving aside His divinity!

The fact is, whether we understand it or not: "The central theme of the Bible is that Jesus is God, and he is also like us, but without sin. Although we can never understand in all its breadth and depth who Jesus really was, Scripture affirms without a doubt that he was divine and human, he was God in human flesh because 'the Word became flesh and dwelt among us' (John 1:14)".[295] That is why, as a True Human Being, Jesus exclaimed from the cross, *I am thirsty.*

Once again, the beloved disciple, the one who stood at the foot of the cross, can with all the certainty of the divine revelation that was bestowed upon him and with the certainty of having been an eyewitness to what the man/God, called Jesus of Nazareth, said while he was crucified; With these two

[293] F. F. Bruce. *The Epistle to the Hebrews.* (Grand Rapids, Michigan. New Creation and William B. Eerdmans Publishing Company. 1987), 86.

[294] Samuel Perez Millos. *Exegetical commentary on the Greek text of the New Testament: HEBREWS.* (Viladecavalls (Barcelona), Spain. Editorial CLIE. 2009),248.

[295] Vallarta. *LIKE HIS BROTHERS IN EVERYTHING* (THE NATURE OF JESUS). (La Habra, California. Internet. Article published on December 11, 2016. Retrieved August 31, 2021), ¿? https://iasdvallarta.org/wp/blog/2016/12/11/semejante-a-sus-hermanos-en-todo-la-naturaleza-de-jesus/

authorities, he was able to say: "After this – after the intense darkness and having begged for the presence of the Father – as Jesus knew that everything had already been fulfilled, and in order for the Scripture to be fulfilled, he said, *'I am thirsty'.*"[296]

This expression clearly shows us the humanity of Jesus Christ. The Crucified One was not a ghost who appeared to suffer on the Cross as some Gnostics have taught. Jesus was a true human being! His pain was as real as ours.

Remember that story that I have told you more than once and that I now repeat in a few words. On one of my missionary trips to the Oaxacan highlands in Mexico, my wife accompanied me. It was the month of May, so the heat was intense. After crossing the river in Ayotzintepec, Oaxaca, we walked in the sweltering heat heading straight to a town called Arroyo Jabalí.

Three hours after I left the river, my wife, Sara Perdomo de Barajas, was thirsty, she could hardly speak anymore. Her tongue was stuck to her palate.

When we reached the edges of the village, there was a small stream. My wife drew strength from I don't know where and ran, got into the creek, and sat inside it to drink water and cool off.

When I saw her already satisfied and fresh, I told her to look up the stream. Oh, nooo! Was her expression. A little late to say the least. Two big pigs were cooling off in the little water that was running![297]

My wife and I only went about four hours without water. Jesus went about eleven or twelve hours without drinking enough water. His thirst was as real as ours on the way to

---

[296]   John 19:28, (DHH).

[297]   Eleazar Barajas. *Water please!* The full story is found in my book: Indigenous Educational Center: The History of the Indigenous Educational Center in the cities of Córdoba, Veracruz and Tuxtepec, Oaxaca, and their missions. Pp.303-308

Arroyo Jabalí. And it was so real because, like us, Jesus was a human being.

II.- NO TO CONFORMISM.

One of the apostle Paul's recommendations to Christians is that they do not live the same as other people live. May they not live like people who do not know Jesus Christ as their personal Savior. The Apostle Paul says: "Therefore, my brethren, I beg you by the mercy of God to present yourselves as a living, holy and pleasing offering to God. This is the true worship you must offer. Do not live by the criteria of the present time anymore; on the contrary, change your way of thinking so that your way of life changes and you come to know the will of God, that is, what is good, what is pleasing to you, what is perfect".[298]

Paul recalls that one of the ideas for the worship of God was sacrifices. Tribes, villages and in some of the cities, sacrifices of animals and even human beings were made – and in some places, still are made. The difference is that Paul does not say that they make sacrifices, but that they make living sacrifice. It does not say that they make a sacrifice as did the ancients and some contemporaries who, after sacrificing the animal, followed their daily lives thinking that they had already fulfilled worshipping their God. Paul calls for a reasonable non-ritualistic sacrifice. For Paul: "Worship that pleases God is an 'informed' sacrifice; that is, the sacrifice offered by the Christian who understands who God is, what He has given us in the Gospel, and what he demands of us".[299]

---

[298] Romans 12:1-2, (NIV).

[299] Douglas J. Moo. *Romans: Commentary with application; from the biblical text to a contemporary application.* (Miami, Florida. Editorial Vida. 2011), 385.

Well, Pastor, and what does this have to do with Jesus' expression on the cross when He said, *I am thirsty*? The lesson I want to share with you is that Jesus, even in the worst circumstances of his life and even in the last minutes of his visible bodily and earthly existence, did not accommodate himself to the culture of his time.

In the Gospel of Mark, we have some words that we must pay a little attention to. Mark said that when Jesus exclaimed, *I am thirsty*, that at that moment: "... they gave him wine mixed with myrrh, but Jesus did not accept it".[300] And, what does that mean? What is the teaching we can learn from this attitude of Jesus? He was thirsty, but he didn't agree to take what he was offered. Why did he reject it?

One idea is that what Jesus was given to drink: "It was not a narcotic drink to mitigate pain..., but wine diluted in water that the workers used to quench thirst".[301] Jesus refused to take what he was offered because in his time the mixing of wine with myrrh was a kind of drug. Those who were crucified were given this drink to help them endure their pain; it was a kind of tranquilizer like morphine, although, I think, wine and myrrh were not as powerful a mixture as morphine. But they believed that wine would dampen their pains.

And here's the lesson. Our society lives such bitter moments that they want to get out of reality, that's why they abuse alcohol, tranquilizer pills, illegal drugs and such in order to escape the situation in which they find themselves. What's wrong with our society? You are looking for your remedy to bitterness in the wrong places! Where do they try to appease their bitterness? Where do you try to fix your pain? You and I know the answers: In addition to alcohol and drugs,

---

[300]   Mark 15:23, (NIV).
[301]   Footnote in *The Bible of the Americas: Study Bible*. (Nashville, Tennessee. Edited by The Lockman Foundation. Published by B&H Publishing Group. 2000), 1493

there are parties, dances and, in some cases, some look to the church for the remedy to their bitterness.

Yes, the church can be a good place to fix bitterness! It can be a good place to help with the evils that haunt us! But, in reality, what they are looking for is an adoration that helps them disconnect from the reality of the world in which they live.

These types of people are not looking for worship to help them confront their everyday problems with the power of Jesus Christ. They are people who have conformed to what society says despite knowing that it will not give them the answer to their emotional and spiritual wounds.

Jesus did not adapt to the culture of his time. He said NO to the conformism of his time. Jesus had to fulfill what was announced by the biblical writers. One of them had prophetically written part of what would happen to the Promised Messiah. He said, "My mouth is dry like a tile; my tongue is stuck to my palate. ... and when I was thirsty, I was given to drink vinegar".[302]

"Psalm 22 arises from a very intense experience of suffering. The one who suffers feels very lonely, abandoned, but he continues to trust in God".[303] It is a prophetic Psalm with emphasis on the sufferings of the Messiah Promised by God to the nation of Israel; it mentions the sufferings that the Messiah went through on the Cross of Mount Calvary. The verse of this Psalm, which is composed of verses 12-18, "is the description of a terrible suffering. ... The very accurate description of what Jesus suffered is striking – notice the prophecy and its fulfillment in Jesus. Many bulls, the evil

---

[302] Psalm 22:15; 69:21, (DHH).

[303] Daniel Carro, José Tomás Poe and Rubén O. Zorzoli (General Editors). *Hispanic World Bible Commentary: Volume 8: PSALMS.* (El Paso, Texas. Editorial Mundo Hispano.2002), 119.

and powerful gathered against him. They stretched his body (vv. 14-17); caused terrible pains in his hands and feet (v.16); **he was very thirsty** (v. 15, cf. Jn. 19:28); they cast lots on his clothes (v.18; cf. John 19:23)".[304]

So, then, this fifth word: The expressive word- *I am thirsty,* makes a clear reference therefore that Jesus Christ was not any kind of ghosts; Jesus was a True Human Being who suffered the terrible pain caused by the blows of the soldiers, the nails, the thorns of the crown, the hunger, the terrible thirst, and the roughness of the wood with which the Cross on which he was crucified was made. Jesus Christ was a True Human Being!

III.- THE RIGHT WAY.

The Evangelist John says that; "Jesus went out carrying his cross, to go to the so-called *'Place of the Skull'* (which in Hebrew is called *Golgotha*). There they crucified him, and with him two others, one on each side, leaving Jesus in the middle".[305] Pontius Pilate had given the order for Jesus' crucifixion and the Roman soldiers executed it. Taking Jesus, says the Evangelist, again outraged him, and after these new insults, they tore off the scarlet mantle with which they had covered him with, put his clothes on him, and carrying the cross on his shoulders, took him to the Calvary to begin the execution against the Holy of Holies.

The road to follow is not always made of roses and beautiful weather, sometimes it is painful, enormous weight,

---

[304]   Daniel Carro, José Tomás Poe and Rubén O. Zorzoli (General Editors). *Hispanic World Bible Commentary: Volume 8: PSALMS.* (El Paso, Texas. Editorial Mundo Hispano.2002), 122. The **Bolds** and *Italics* are mine.

[305]   John 19:17-18, (DHH).

abuse, unbridled hatred, mountains to climb with a heavy load; sometimes the right way is death!

Pastor, isn't this an irony when God offers us peace, abundant life, and well-being? Yes, it's an irony! But that is still a reality in the Christian life. God desires the best for us, but sometimes we must learn what God's discipline is; we must go through what we don't understand. Jesus Christ did understand it very well. He did not walk to the Calvary without knowing the reason towards the death on the Cross.

He came to the top of the mountain and allowed himself to be crucified because he knew that in this way the correct path that we Christians should follow would already be less burdensome, because he walks it with us.

It was there, then, on the Calvary, that Jesus, in his terrible agony, said, *I am thirsty*. Jesus thirsted so that we, instead of living with unsatiated spiritual thirst, may receive an abundant life; a life of freshness and refreshment with the spiritual water provided by the Redeemer of our souls. Jesus had said to the Samaritan woman, "But whoever drinks of the water which I will give him shall never thirst; but the water that I will give him will be in him a fountain of water that leaps for eternal life".[306] Sometime later he said to his first followers, "I have come so they may have life, and that they may have it abundantly".[307]

CONCLUSION.

When Jesus said, *I am thirsty,* he showed all his humanity. He was a true human being. Physical thirst is a desire that must be satisfied, otherwise, in addition to the agony felt by not drinking water, you also run the risk of dying dehydrated.

---

[306] John 4:14, (KJV,1960).
[307] John 10:10, (KJV, 1960).

Spiritual thirst is also a desire of the soul that must be satisfied, otherwise one runs the risk of continually living in spiritual despair; one runs the risk of living with a dry mouth for lack of God's blessings.

In the walk of the Christian life, the best example to follow, the right path is the example left to us by Jesus Christ. He refused to escape the pain, refused to take the vinegar and wine blended, refused to be overcome by cowardice, he knew that the only way to overcome the problems was to face them.

The expression, *I am thirsty*, was not only to fulfill the Scriptures, but it was also so that you and I would never suffer from spiritual thirst.

¡Amen!

DECLARATION OF VICTORY

-The sixth word: The guaranteed word- "Consummated is"
John 19:30

INTRODUCTION.

With this expression: *It is finished,* "Jesus' suffering ends and God's plan for the salvation of mankind is fulfilled (John 4:34; 17:4)".[308] Jesus Christ had achieved victory! The Holy Bible says, *It is finished.*[309] *It is finished,* or as others translate, everything is already complete: "'Everything is already complete' is just a word in Greek, *tetélestai*; and Jesus died with a cry of triumph on his lips. He did not say, 'It's all over,' as if acknowledging His defeat; but proclaiming His victory with a cry of jubilation. He seemed to be shattered on the Cross. But He knew He had won the victory".[310] In the midst of all that suffering, I can say; Wonderful! Yes, wonderful! Gratifying and comforting because the Lord opened the door of salvation!

---

[308] Footnote in *the Schematic Study Bible.* (Brazil. United Bible Societies. 2010), 1601.

[309] *Holy Bible. Red Letter Edition.* (Chicago, Illinois. The John A. Hertel CO. 1960), 657.

[310] William Barclay. *Commentary on the New Testament: Volume 6: JOHN: II.* (Terrassa (Barcelona), Spain. Editorial CLIE. 1996), 293.

It is finished teaches that: "The Cross was finished. Nothing pending, nothing to solve. God had accomplished the work of redemption in the Divine-human person of His only begotten Son".[311]

It is finished, is therefore the cry of victory! Victory over what? was the victory over three important acts and effects of God for the benefit of mankind. I invite you to notice these acts of victory.

I.- IT WAS VICTORY OVER SIN!

It is finished: It was a cry of triumph over sin. "On the cross Jesus won victory over sin. ... With this victory, now nothing ties us to sin, and, on the contrary, it advances us in the certainty that we are called to overcome. Christ overcame and made us victorious!"[312] "According to Isaiah, the Servant of the Lord, he somehow bore all the problems and pains we inflict on ourselves as a result of living according to our purposes and not God's". [313] This is, Jesus Christ bore the punishment that was ours and, in that way, the Lord Jesus received the judgment caused by our own moral faults. More realistically, these moral faults the Bible calls sin.

But now there is victory over sin! The Saving Work of Jesus was sealed. Human beings who are still spiritually lost now could be saved. Jesus Christ obeyed the Father even in the most critical events of His earthly ministry and now,

---

[311] Samuel Pérez Millos. *Comentario exegético al texto griego del Nuevo Testamento: JUAN.* (Viladecavalls (Barcelona), España. Editorial CLIE. 2016), 1713.

[312] Fernando Alexis Jimenez. *Jesus Christ overcame on the cross and gave us victory.* (La Habra, California. Internet. Article published on April 13, 2017. Retrieved September 7, 2021), ¿? http://www.mensajerodelapalabra.com/site/index.php/ jesucristo-vencio-en-la-cruz-y-nos-dio-la-victoria/ .

[313] Mitch. Glaser, *Isaiah 53: An Explanation. This chapter will change your life.* (New York, USA. Chosen People Productions. 2010), 65

when He has already overcome sin, God Himself has declared Him God with power. It is not that he was not, but now, with his victory over sin on the Cross of the Calvary, he presents himself as the victorious God.

In Peter's speech at the inauguration of the Christian Church in the city of Jerusalem, Peter, from the Upper Room, told the Jews who had gathered to celebrate the Feast of Pentecost: "Know all the people of Israel, with all assurance, that this same Jesus whom you crucified, God has made him Lord and Messiah" (Lord and Christ – KJ.60).[314]

Jesus' victory over sin has shown that evil is not absolute; Jesus has shown that it is possible to live in communion with God. That is, with the perfect obedience that Jesus showed to the Father until that day when he cried out with all his strength: "It is finished!", Jesus Christ, not only obtained the victory over sin, but also led humanity to the bosom of the Father. Today we can have fellowship with God!

The victory over sin made by Jesus Christ has also made him an intermediary between God and humanity. The author of the Book of Hebrews says that: "Therefore, since we have a great High Priest who entered heaven, Jesus the Son of God, let us cling to what we believe. Our High Priest understands our weaknesses, because he faced every trial we face, yet he never sinned. So let us approach with all confidence the throne of our God's grace. There we will receive his mercy and find the grace that will help us when we need it most".[315] The New Testament presents Jesus Christ ministering in his three professions: Prophet, Priest, and King. At his first coming, he presented himself as a prophet; in his earthly ministry, he spoke with God, proclaimed God, taught his

---

[314]   Acts 2:36, (DHH).
[315]   Hebrews 4:14-16, (NLT).

disciples, and prophesied. "In the latter part of His earthly ministry, He began to offer Himself to God, which ended up on the Cross, where He offered Himself as a sacrifice for God in our place. Thus, He fulfilled His function as a priest, and from that point on, this has been His function".[316]

Notice that the biblical account says that Jesus, as the high priest he is now, *faced with every trial that we face*. He did it all out of love for us! Contemplating the history or scene of the Calvary, we can see the flag of love waving eternally on the mast that God placed it, there we see it with spiritual eyes "between heaven and earth, there it is on a cross, infamous for men, reconciling to God, glorious for the believer. The debt of sin has been extinguished and there is no longer, nor can there be, any condemnation for those who believe and accept by faith what God has done in Christ".[317] Out of love, Jesus Christ, with his cry, "*It is finished*," defeated the power of sin and gave us freedom from evil power. The debt was paid!

In Christ we are victorious over sin! Jesus' cry of victory on the Cross of the Calvary tells man that the abyss that sin had created between God and humanity: It no longer exists! Jesus Christ has made a spiritual bridge between earth and heaven; a bridge where humanity can walk towards God. Jesus Christ had rightly said that He was the Way. A path that has a bridge over the same abyss that allows a point of contact between divinity and the human race.

Jesus' expression, *It is finished*, is not only the victory over sin, but it is also the defeat of evil. One of the consequences of sin is evil. This entails suffering, pain, anguish, despair, hatred, quarrels, jealousy, envy, injustice, death and things alike. With

---

[316] Witness Lee. *The heavenly ministry of Christ*. (Anaheim, California. Living Stream Ministry www.ism.org. 2003), 63.

[317] Samuel Perez Millos. *Exegetical commentary on the Greek text of the New Testament: JOHN*. (Viladecavalls (Barcelona), Spain. Editorial CLIE. 2016), 1713.

Jesus' cry, *It is finished,* all of this has no power over those of us who are in Christ Jesus. He has overcome evil! Hope has triumphed over despair; righteousness has overcome sin.

Finished is "was and is the atonement of sin, toward God".[318] This is that, with the expression or cry of the Crucified One, he has revealed divine justice to such a degree that it is now possible to be saved from sin and evil by grace. The victory is already won! So, right now, salvation by grace is completely free, its price has already been paid; Salvation in Christ Jesus is a divine gift to that person who believes in Jesus Christ as His Savior and His Lord. *It's finished*!

II.- IT WAS VICTORY OVER DEATH!

Listen to these Pauline words: "For the corruptible must be clothed with the incorruptible, and the mortal, with immortality. When the corruptible is revolved in the incorruptible, and the mortal, immortality, then what is written will be fulfilled: 'Death has been devoured by victory'. 'Where is your victory, O death? Where is your sting, O death?' The sting of death is sin, and the power of sin is the law. But thank God, who gives us victory through our Lord Jesus Christ!"[319] Magnificent declaration of the power of the Risen One! A statement that leaves no doubt that the Resurrection of Jesus: Was the victory over death!

It is a writing in which we must note, "first, the two demonstrative pronouns, this, which points to the mortal and corruptible framework of the human being. Second, the Greek word *phtharton* which means that which is subject

---

[318] B. H Carroll. *Bible Commentary: The Four Gospels.* Volume 6. Volume II. Trd. Sara A. Hale. (Terrassa (Barcelona), Spain. Editorial CLIE. 1986), 459

[319] I Corinthians 15:53-57, (NIV).

to decay or destruction applied to mortal man. Third, the verb *must*, denotes the need that God imposes and acts as an auxiliary verb to be clothed".[320] The fundamental idea is that believers in Christ Jesus should be clothed by God with immortality free from all contamination. It is clear to the apostle Paul that this is a work of God. This is part of the result of the victory over death accomplished by Christ Jesus with His Resurrection.

The fact of being clothed with immortality is because "as we are, we have no possibility of inheriting the kingdom of God. We may be well equipped to face the life of this world, but we are not well equipped for the life of the world to come".[321]

In the previous section we talked about how Jesus Christ, by uttering his declaration of victory: *It is finished!* put an end to the power of sin. Now, the apostle Paul, continues with this same idea, because the words that we have read in I Corinthians 15:53, refer to the idea that, being in Christ, we are free from sin by the victory of Christ on the Calvary, but also, *It is finished,* refers to an eschatological transformation. That is, "This text (I Cor.15:53) not only communicates the message that believers will be transformed, but also implies a certain discontinuity with the past".[322] We must no longer be and will not be the same! Christ's victory on the Cross has led us believers in Him to a new dimension.

Pastor, what do you mean when you talk about being in a New Dimension? I was told that: "A person has to change to enter another level of life; and Paul insists that we have

---

[320]   Simon J. Kistemaker. *Commentary on the New Testament: I Corinthians.* (Grand Rapids, Michigan. Challenge Books. Published by Baker Book House. 1998), 636-637.

[321]   William Barclay. *Commentary on the New Testament: Volume 9: CORINTHIANS.* (Terrassa (Barcelona), Spain. Editorial CLIE. 1996), 194.

[322]   Simon J. Kistemaker. *Commentary on the New Testament: I Corinthians.* (Grand Rapids, Michigan. Challenge Books. Published by Baker Book House. 1998), 637.

to undergo a radical transformation to enter the kingdom of God".[323] A radical transformation that has begun with: *"It is finished"*. In this way, believers in Christ Jesus, in this new dimension, are holy to God. We are not by our own effort but because it is part of the result of: *It is finished.* That is, we are saints because *it is Finished:* It was victory over death!

It is Finished does not lead to the book of Revelation where we read that: "Everyone who has ears to hear must listen to the Spirit and understand what he says to the churches. Those who come out victorious will not suffer harm from the second death".[324] Why? Because life has triumphed over death! If death has been overcome, then for Christians, the fear of death should no longer be torment. The love of Jesus Christ and the love for the Lord must remove all fear of death: "For this Jesus gave us the victory over death, banishing his fear with the wonder of God's love".[325]

So, *It is finished*, "announce that the days of death are numbered".[326] Victory over death has brought about or produced life now and for eternity.

III.- IT WAS THE VICTORY OVER SATAN!

Jesus was in the synagogue on a Sabbath, as was his custom, he went to the synagogue to study the Scriptures together with the Jewish population. On that day, there was a woman who had been hunched over for eighteen years. "She

---

[323] William Barclay. *Commentary on the New Testament: Volume 9: CORINTHIANS.* (Terrassa (Barcelona), Spain. Editorial CLIE. 1996), 195.

[324] Revelation 2:11, (NLT).

[325] William Barclay. *Commentary on the New Testament: Volume 9: CORINTHIANS.* (Terrassa (Barcelona), Spain. Editorial CLIE. 1996), 196.

[326] Simon J. Kistemaker. (Grand Rapids, Michigan. Challenge Books. Published by Baker Book House. 1998), 637

apparently suffered from a certain type of bone degeneration or muscle paralysis".[327] Jesus healed her and immediately the pastor of the synagogue was angry because Jesus healed her on the Sabbath or the day of Rest.

To the response of the anger and words of that man and the attendees of the meeting in that synagogue: "Jesus responded sternly, addressing those who agreed with the head of the synagogue as hypocrites",[328] he said to them: "Hypocrites! Doesn't each of you untie your ox or donkey on the Sabbath, and take it out of the barn to take it to drink water? However, to this woman, who is Abraham's daughter, and whom Satan had bound for eighteen long years, were her chains not to be taken away on the Sabbath?"[329] Another version translates verse sixteen this way: "And this one, who is the daughter of Abraham, whom Satan has been bound for eighteen long years, should not be freed from this bond on the Sabbath?"[330]

Jesus' answer also teaches that when Jesus cried out: *Tetelestai*; *It is finished*, provides victory over Satan himself because in this example of healing in which the duration of the disease is mentioned and emphasized that it was bound by Satan. The cruelty of this enemy is very noticeable in this woman. "In this culture, being a woman and suffering from this ailment makes her doubly marginalized".[331] She was doubly tied up! One for culture and the other for Satan. But he was freed from both ties! Christ Jesus' final victory over Satan was approaching. Its culmination was when Jesus cried out, *It is finished*.

---

[327] Darrell L. Bock. *Bible Commentary with Application: LUCAS. From the biblical text to a contemporary application*. (Miami, Florida. Editorial Vida. 2011), 341.

[328] Darrell L. Bock. *Bible Commentary with Application: LUCAS. From the biblical text to a contemporary application*. (Miami, Florida. Editorial Vida. 2011), 341.

[329] Luke 13:15-16, (NIV).

[330] Luke 13:16, (KJV, 1960).

[331] Darrell L. Bock. *Bible Commentary with Application: LUCAS. From the biblical text to a contemporary application*. (Miami, Florida. Editorial Vida. 2011), 341.

The Lord Jesus has been calling the nation of Israel to repent. For the reaction of the person in charge of the Synagogue. - verse 15 -, we understand that they had not yet repented or understood what the authority and ministry of Jesus Christ had. "A second theme of this passage is the description of a battle against Satan, the source of the woman's misfortune".[332] And, not only of her but of all humanity. "According to Luke, this is the second healing that Jesus did on the Sabbath. The first is in Luke 6:6-11. There is a third that appears in Luke 14:1-6".[333] In each of them it is noted that Jesus Christ had the power to overcome Satan. However, his culmination came when he said, *It is finished*. There, on the Cross of the Calvary, Jesus put an end to satanic power.

"Before He created human beings, God created an innumerable host of spirits called angels".[334] Among them Satan was created. He was the most powerful and privileged spirit of all the others. His name is Lucifer, a name that means the shining being. "This brilliant angel was described thus: 'the seal of perfection, full of wisdom, and finished with beauty' (Ezekiel 28:12). Apart from Jesus Christ, no one has been as powerful as Satan. No one has been as full of wisdom as this enemy of God and Christians. He had the audacity to use his wisdom against Jesus Christ and put him to the test.[335]

So, Jesus' cry of victory on the Cross was a cry of victory of worldwide and eternal scope. *It is Finished* assures us of victory over the author of sin, which is Satan and his demons

---

[332] Darrell L. Bock. *Comentarios Bíblicos con Aplicación: LUCAS. Del texto bíblico a una aplicación contemporánea.* (Miami, Florida. Editorial Vida. 2011), 340.

[333] Commentary on *The Schematic Study Bible.* (Brazil. United Bible Societies. 2010), 1527.

[334] P.S. Bramsen. *One God a message: Discover the mystery: Make the old man.* (Grand Rapids, Michigan. Editorial Portavoz, a subsidiary of Kregel Publications. 2011), 117.

[335] Matthew 4:1-11; Mark. 1.12-13; Luke. 4.1-13.

and, since sin is the originator of death,[336] then victory over Satan is also victory over sin and death. *It is finished*, is a victory against all that is evil; against everything that is harmful to physical health, to the economy, to social relations and, of course, to the spiritual field. For this and much more, *"Consummated is"*, it was and is a great victory! A great victory against Satan!

It is finished is, therefore, a cry of victory over Satan himself and over all hosts of evil. He is already defeated, Jesus Christ overcame him on the Cross, although he is still deceiving and annoying Christians, the apostle Paul says that: God the Father, based on Jesus' victory over Satan: "... the God of peace will soon crush Satan under your feet". The King James Version says, "And the God of peace will shortly crush Satan under your feet".[337] Charles Spurgeon, the prince of preachers rejoiced in this Pauline promise saying, "'SHORTLY'. Happy word! We will soon crush the ancient snake! What a joy it is to crush evil! What dishonor it is for Satan to be crushed by human feet! Let us crush the tempter under our feet through faith in Jesus".[338] We can do this because with the cry of victory: *It is finished*, our Savior Jesus Christ, gives us all the authority to do so because, He overcame him on the Cross! Satan is a defeated being for all eternity!

CONCLUSION.

It is finished is Jesus' great cry of victory on the Cross. It was the cry of victory against sin, against death, and against

[336] Romans 6:23, (DHH). The payment that sin gives is death, but God's gift is eternal life in union with Christ Jesus, our Lord.

[337] Romans 16:20, (DHH and KJ, 1960).

[338] Charles Spurgeon. *Devotional: It will soon crush Satan.* (La Habra, California. Internet. Retrieved September 21, 2021), ¿? https://atalayas21.com/2-aplastara-en-breve-a-satanas/

Satan. The apostle Paul was very sure of this triple victory, so he said: "For I am convinced that neither death nor life, nor angels nor demons, nor the present nor what is to come, nor the powers, nor the high nor the deep, nor anything in all creation can separate us from the love that God has manifested to us in Christ Jesus our Lord".[339] This is present and eternal security, thanks to the triumph of Jesus on the Cross of the Calvary.

So, with the cry, *It is finished*, "the atonement was made for sin; ... The Substitute Vicar of sinners died for them".[340] Death no longer has power over Christians, Satan has to ask God for permission to cause us harm, and salvation triumphed over condemnation.

Everything was fully satisfied! *It is finished!* It was all finished!

---

[339]   Romans 8:38-39, (DHH).

[340]   B. H Carroll. *Bible Commentary: The Four Gospels. Volume 6. Volume II.* Trd. Sara A. Hale. (Terrassa (Barcelona), Spain. Editorial CLIE. 1986), 460.

FAITHFUL FULFILLMENT

The seventh word: The word of trust- "Father,
into your hands I commend my spirit."
Luke 23:46.

INTRODUCTION.

Jesus Christ, still aware of what he is doing, after the great spiritual battle amid darkness and abandonment of his Father, has spoken the other two words we have analyzed: *"I am thirsty"* and *"It is finished"*. And, shortly before the time comes for the Passover Sacrifice, Jesus, the Lamb of God, again in a loud voice, says, *"Father, into your hands I commend my spirit"*.

In the magazine The Digital Phoenician, a Palliative Care worker says that his patients were people who were sent home to die. In those last days of life, patients confessed to the specialist their frustrations; they regrated the kind of life they had led. The specialist wrote five regrets his patients had before they were about to die. Here are those five regrets:

1. I wish I had the courage to live a life true to myself, not the life that others expected of me. Looking back, the dying man realizes how many dreams he failed to fulfill. It all depends on the choices that are made while one has health.

2. I wish I hadn't worked so hard. They lost the childhood and youth of their children and the company of their partner. Most of their life was spent away from home.

3. I wish I had the courage to express my feelings. They never became what they really were; they repressed their feelings to keep the peace. They lived a mediocre life.

4. I would have liked to have been in contact with my friends. It is common for anyone in a busy lifestyle to let friendships disappear. And when it comes to dying, it dies without them.

5. I would have liked to allow myself to be happier. Happiness is a choice; something that many understand in their last hours of life.

Remember: Life is a choice. It's your life. Choose consciously, choose wisely, choose honestly. Choose happiness![341]

What do we notice in these regrets?

What we can see in these five cries of the dying are expressions of defeat: expressions of frustration and unattainable longings.

---

[341] The Vanguard. "(La Habra, California. Internet. Retrieved March 29, 2021), ¿? https://www.lavanguardia.com/vida/20111214/54240193062/los-cinco-lamentos-moribundos.html

What happened to Jesus Christ?

Quite the opposite was with the death of the Crucified, in His case, it was a death of victory and not regrets or frustrations. Although at least seven expressions came out of his mouth, none of them show defeat; they show no frustration or unreached longings. Moreover, in his penultimate expression, Jesus Christ showed: A declaration of victory! And, in the seventh declaration, Jesus Christ, is confident that he has faithfully fulfilled his Redemptive Mission.

I.- FAITHFUL REPRESENTATION.

Having faithfully fulfilled in the world, what was left for Jesus to do? Only to invoke the Father to restore him to his side; to the place it had always had, even before the world was created. He asked him to fulfill the plea he had made to him in John 17:5, which says, "And now, Father, glorify me in your presence with the glory I had with you before the world existed".[342]

We notice in the account in Luke 23:46 that Jesus calls God father again. He does it intimately and personally. He probably used the Aramaic word: *Abba. Into your hands I commend my spirit* an expression found in Psalm 31:5. "That prayer was the one uttered by a Jewish child at bedtime at night. Jesus made the prayer even more tender by adding the word Father (ABBA) to it. Even on the cross, death was for Jesus like falling asleep in the arms of his Father".[343]

---

[342]   John 17:5, (NIV).

[343]   William Barclay. *Commentary on the New Testament: Volume 4: LUKE.* (Terrassa (Barcelona), Spain. Editorial CLIE. 1994), 346.

The apostle Paul told the brethren of Rome that all who are led by the Spirit of God are children of God and that they "did not receive a spirit that again enslaves them to fear, but the Spirit who adopts them as children and allows them to cry out, '*Abba*! Father!'."[344] It is therefore an intimate relationship: A relationship of love and affection.

While Jesus mentions this expression, he is fulfilling a Levitical prophecy. It was three o'clock in the afternoon when Jesus said, *"Father, into your hands I commend my spirit"*, and then he died. That was the exact hour of the sacrifice of the Passover Lamb. It was the sacrifice that commemorated the Passover and the Atonement of sin.

So, Jesus, by saying, *"Father, into your hands I commend my spirit"*, was faithfully fulfilling the mission he had cast upon himself: to save mankind from its sins.

II.- HE NEVER FAINTED!

The evangelist Matthew says that Jesus, "'Cried out again with force'. This was a sign that, after all his pains and fatigues, his life was still whole in him, and his nature, strong".[345] Demonic forces and human forces failed to weaken the Crucified One to such a degree that he could not speak. We know that one of the first things that abandons a dying man is the voice. You may be aware; he can hear what we say to him and can still see clearly, but the voice abandons him; in moments of agony, he cannot express what he feels or what he wants. "But Christ, precisely at his expiration, spoke as one who has been in the power of all his strength.

---

[344] Romans 8:14'15, (NIV).
[345] Matthew Henry. *Exegetical-Devotional Commentary on the Entire Bible: Matthew.* Td. Francisco Lacueva. (Terrassa (Barcelona), Spain. Editorial CLIE. 1984), 551.

What is the lesson for us? It is a lesson given to us to understand that it was not life that left him, but that it was he who gave permission to death to approach him".[346]

In addition, we note that Jesus' cry in his last moments of earthly life was an event that marked an end to the dominion of sin. That is to say: "The cry of Christ on the cross was like a trumpet calling for the withdrawal of all other sacrifices".[347] A trumpet voice announcing that the Lamb of God was dying to deliver humans from the sin that was enslaving them.

III.- "HE GAVE THE SPIRIT".

This is an expression that in one way or another, the four evangelists, recognized as the highest authority of divine revelation, they assure it as a true fact.

> *The evangelist Matthew said, *"He gave up the spirit"*.
> *Mark said that Jesus, *"Expired"*.
> Dr. Luke said, *"Then Jesus, crying out with a loud voice, said, Father, into your hands I commend my spirit. And having said this, he expired"*.
> And John, the beloved disciple, said that Jesus *"gave up the spirit"*.[348]

The apostle John was there on the Calvary, he heard the words of Jesus directly; he was an eyewitness to what

---

[346] Matthew Henry. *Exegetical-Devotional Commentary on the Entire Bible: Matthew.* Td. Francisco Lacueva. (Terrassa (Barcelona), Spain. Editorial CLIE. 1984), 551.

[347] Matthew Henry. *Exegetical-Devotional Commentary on the Entire Bible: Matthew.* Td. Francisco Lacueva. (Terrassa (Barcelona), Spain. Editorial CLIE. 1984), 551

[348] Matthew 27:50; Mark 15:37; Luke 23:46; John 19:30, (KJV, 1960).

Christ Jesus said. The others received this message by divine revelation. So, in both cases, we have a true historical fact that announces that Jesus Christ really died.

We are, therefore, talking about the death of a mere mortal. In the Bible passage we are reading, "It is striking that the term spirit (*ruah*) is used instead of soul or life (*nefesh*)".[349] That is, the evangelists gave this incident a spiritual tone rather than a simple death of a human being. It was the death of the Lamb of God who takes away the sin of the world![350]

John 19:30 says that Jesus: "*... he bowed his head and surrendered the spirit*".[351] And what does this mean? It is said that those who have died first die and then bow their heads, but Jesus first bowed his head and then gave up the spirit. This is, Jesus, after all that He had done, after His Faithful Fulfillment, invited death to come to Him.

Let us listen to Jesus Christ, when he told his listeners that he was the good shepherd: "That is why the Father loves me: because I give my life to receive it again. No one takes it from me, but I hand it over of my own free will. I have the authority to deliver it, and I also have the authority to receive it again".[352]

Wonderful and excellent prophetic passage! It is one of those passages that encapsulates the purpose of the Redemptive Mission of Jesus Christ. He came to give his life as a ransom for the price of sin. What do these words of Jesus tell us? They tell us the main theological ideas:

---

[349]   Eduardo G Nelson, Mervin Breneman, Ricardo Souto Copeiro and others. *Hispanic World Bible Commentary: Psalms: Volume 8*. (El Paso, Texas. Editorial Mundo Hispano. 2002), 143.

[350]   John 1:29.

[351]   John 19:30, (NIV).

[352]   John 10:17-18, (NIV).

1. "We are told that – Jesus – saw his whole life as an act of obedience to God".[353] So when he came to the cross and pronounced, *"Into your hands I commend my spirit"*, it is as if he were saying to the Father, "I have faithfully fulfilled what you entrusted to me".

2. The words of Jesus: "They tell us that Jesus always saw the cross and glory as inseparable".[354] What we notice is that Jesus never lost the vision and assurance that his Father would never abandon him, that he would always be by his side.

This trust or assurance of Jesus gives us a great lesson that says, "Life is all worthwhile even though things come at a price. You always have to pay a price to get them".[355] Nothing that is of value is free, even the salvation of our life came at a great price. mechanics, artists, professionals, athletes, builders, philosophers, theologians, writers and even housewives have all paid a price for what they are doing.

Now, think about this: "No one can enter heaven, no one can be in God's presence unless they pay the price of obedience and submission to the Lordship of Jesus Christ. You must pay a price! Salvation is free, Jesus Christ has already paid for it, but to obtain and live that salvation, you must pay a price! Jesus Christ faithfully fulfilled his Mission and therefore with all confidence and security, he said: "In your hands I commend my spirit".[356]

---

[353] William Barclay. *Commentary on the New Testament: Volume 6: JOHN: II.* (Terrassa (Barcelona), Spain. Editorial CLIE. 1996), 85.

[354] William Barclay. *Commentary on the New Testament: Volume 6: JOHN: II.* (Terrassa (Barcelona), Spain. Editorial CLIE. 1996), 85.

[355] William Barclay. *Commentary on the New Testament: Volume 6: JOHN: II.* (Terrassa (Barcelona), Spain. Editorial CLIE. 1996), 85.

[356] Luke 23:46, (NIV).

CONCLUSION.

Take this into account, "Jesus Christ did not lose his life, but gave it up. The cross was not imposed on him: he accepted it voluntarily... for us".[357] He said, "Father, into your hands I commend my spirit".[358] It is a statement that "reflects the trust that Jesus has in the Father... he trusts that the Lord will take care of him".[359] This is a clear example that, if we trust God, he will always take care of us now and for eternity.

If you give your spirit or your life to the Lord Jesus Christ, God the Father will always take care of you. You will always have eternal life together with Jesus Christ!

Amen!

---

[357]   William Barclay. *Commentary on the New Testament: Volume 6: JOHN: II.* (Terrassa (Barcelona), Spain. Editorial CLIE. 1996), 85.

[358]   Luke 23:46, (NIV).

[359]   Darrell L. Bock. *Bible Commentary with Application: LUCAS. From the biblical text to a contemporary application.* (Miami, Florida. Editorial Vida. 2011), 545.

A NEW PATH

"At that moment the veil of the temple was
torn in two, from top to bottom".
Matthew 27:51, (DHH).

INTRODUCTION.

At the very moment when Jesus Christ gave the spirit to the
Father, the veil of the temple was torn into two parts. The
account that the evangelist Matthew makes in these three
verses – 51-53 – of chapter 27 of his Gospel, are tremendous
miracles.

Matthew says that "the veil of the temple was torn in two,
from top – down". "As in other miracles of Christ – in this
one – a mystery was enclosed".[360] A mystery that presents the
door of the beginning of the New Path.

What does this mystery teach us?

---

[360] Matthew Henry. *Exegetical-Devotional Commentary on the Entire Bible: Matthew.*
Td. Francisco Lacueva. (Terrassa (Barcelona), Spain. Editorial CLIE. 1984), 551.

I.- SYMBOL OF THE DEATH OF CHRIST.

The Evangelist Matthew said that at the moment Jesus died on the Cross of the Calvary: "... the veil of the temple was torn in two, from top to bottom". This is an expression, or very short account, that the Evangelist Matthew mentions in his Gospel; it is a proclamation that is also found in the Gospel of Mark and Luke. The three relate in a very short way this story, or mystery.[361]

It is an expression that refers to a great miracle, a miracle that manifests or reveals one of the mysteries of Salvation in Christ Jesus and that had been, in mysterious form, written in some of the pages of the Old Testament. "Therefore, this expression is inserted into a carousel of events of a 'theophanic' nature (manifestation of God) that frame Jesus' last breath. It is precisely here, in the evangelical context, that the 'tearing' of the veil of the temple is introduced".[362] A symbol of the death of Christ Jesus.

According to some observers or eyewitnesses, "a wooden partition separated the Holy of Holies from the Holy; and above the door hung the veil, which was torn in two, from top to bottom when the road to the most holy place was opened on Golgotha".[363] Indicating that the death of Jesus inaugurated the New Path to God.

The Evangelist Luke says that "the veil of the temple was torn in half".[364] Mark, like Matthew, says that "the veil of the temple was torn in two from top to bottom".[365] The expression:

---

361   Matthew 27:51; Mark 15:38; Luke 23:45.

362   Giovanna Cheli. *What was the "veil of the temple" that was torn when Jesus died?* (La Habra, California. Internet. Retrieved April 15, 2021), ¿? https://es.aleteia. org/2015/05/26/que-era-el-velo-del-templo-que-se-rasgo-al-morir-jesus/

363   Alfred Edersheim. *The Temple: His ministry and services in the time of Christ.* (Terrassa (Barcelona), Spain. Editorial CLIE. 1990), 68.

364   Luke 23:45, (KJV, 1960).

365   Mark 15:38, (KJV, 1960).

From top to bottom, "indicates that it was not a person who tore the curtain – it was the same God who initiated a New Way for humanity. Hebrews 9:12 and 10:20-29 explain what this means for the Christian",[366] The inauguration of a New Path!

So, we can rightly say that the symbol is very dense, because in Scripture "high" is the place of divine transcendence and "low" instead is the abode of human reality. There is already a New and Unique Way to the Father!

II.- DISCOVERY OF THE MYSTERIES OF THE OLD TESTAMENT.

The tearing of the veil in the Jewish temple was one of the great ancient testamentary mysteries. No one knew anything clearly about this mystery. God had kept it to himself as if it were a secret of Old Testament revelation. It was a secret or literary mystery that none of the ancestors emphasized in this incident, although, mysteriously, the Lord had said to Abraham, "Through you all the families of the earth will be blessed!"[367] How would they be blessed? The mystery was in the death of the Lamb of God and, when this happened, the veil of the Temple was torn announcing that the time had come when the entire human race could be blessed in the forgiveness of sins done by Christ on the Cross of the Calvary.

All the furniture in the Tabernacle contained an eschatological explanation. They all symbolized God's Reconciling Ministry with human beings. All! This includes the veil that divided the Holy Place from the Most Holy Place.

---

[366] Footnote commentary on *the Schematic Study Bible*. (Brazil. United Bible Societies. 2010), 1481

[367] Genesis 12:3, (NIV).

from the desert lands, during the pilgrimage of the Israelites to the Promised Land, the Lord indicated to the people that He was most Holy, and that man was a sinner, therefore, there would be a continuous separation between God and mankind. A great veil in the Tabernacle of Moses served as a symbol of that radical separation.

When King Solomon built the Temple in the city of Jerusalem, he had a veil or a "curtain made of purple linen cloth, and had wings embroidered on it".[368] It can be noted that it was a work of extreme beauty and of great value.

Now, "the temple that King Solomon built for the Lord was twenty-seven meters long by nine meters wide and thirteen and a half meters high".[369] These measurements tell us that: "The temple itself was not very large. It was built not so much as a meeting place of the people, but as the dwelling place of God".[370]

So, then, why did God command to put a veil between His dwelling place and the activities of the priests? "The veil of the temple was there to hide, for it was very serious the punishment that hung over every person who saw the trousseau (furniture, clothes, etc.) of the Most Holy Place, except the high priest – who once a year – with great ceremony and through a cloud of glory and incest",[371] entered that Place with the risk of dying. We are therefore talking about a strong and terrible one: Separation between God and the human being.

Someone asked themselves this question: What was the significance of the veil of the temple being torn in two when Jesus died? In response, we say that: "During the time of Jesus'

---

[368]   2 Chronicles 3:14, (DHH).

[369]   I Kings 6:2, (NIV).

[370]   Footnote commentary on *the Schematic Study Bible*. (Brazil. United Bible Societies. 2010), 492

[371]   Matthew Henry. *Exegetical-Devotional Commentary on the Entire Bible: Matthew*. Td. Francisco Lacueva. (Terrassa (Barcelona), Spain. Editorial CLIE. 1984), 552.

life, the holy temple in Jerusalem was the center of Jewish religious life. This was the place where animal sacrifices and worship were carried out, strictly in accordance with the law of Moses, which was faithfully followed. Hebrews 9:1-9 tells us that in the temple there was a veil that separated the Most Holy Place – the earthly place where God's presence dwelt – from the rest of the temple where men dwelt. This meant that man was separated from God by sin (Isaiah 59:1-2). Only the high priest was allowed to pass behind the veil once a year (Exodus 30:10; Hebrews 9:7), to enter into God's presence throughout Israel and make atonement for their sins (Leviticus 16)".[372]

The tearing of the veil is thus one of the profound theological pronunciations within Christianity. "To give an idea of the extraordinary fact, the Jewish historian Giuseppe Flavio said that not even two horses attached to this great curtain would have been able to break it. Its maintenance was really a venture: it was 20 meters high and ten centimeters thick, to be able to roll it was said that about seventy men were needed".[373]

There was no simple way to approach God; the separation between God and human beings was something very real. The veil symbolized this separation. Now, "When Jesus died, the veil of the temple was torn from top to bottom, illustrating that God, in Christ, abolished the barrier that separated humanity from the divine presence".[374] So, with the tearing

---

[372] Got Questions. *What was the significance of the temple veil being torn in two when Jesus died?* (La Habra, California. Internet. Retrieved April 14, 2021), ¿¿, https://www.gotquestions.org/espanol/velo-templo-rasgado.html

[373] Giovanna Cheli. *What was the "veil of the temple" that was torn when Jesus died?* (La Habra, California. Internet. Retrieved April 15, 2021), ¿? https://es.aleteia.org/2015/05/26/que-era-el-velo-del-templo-que-se-rasgo-al-morir-jesus

[374] Leticia S. Calcada. General Edition. *Holman Illustrated Bible Dictionary.* (Nashville, Tennessee. B&H Publishing Group. 2008), 1618.

of the veil, theology changes, now: "Jesus' compassionate disposition invites us to develop an intimate relationship with God and makes such intimacy possible".[375] It does so by having inaugurated a New Path.

The tearing of the veil in the temple in Jerusalem, the religious center of Judaism made possible the discovery of the mysteries of the Old Testament, while also marking the beginning of a New Path to reach the presence of God.

III.- PRESENTATION OF UNION.

"*The veil was torn from top to bottom*", says evangelist Matthew. The apostle Paul says the same thing, in other words giving theological meaning to this insignificant, but at the same time important event. He says that with the death of Jesus Christ a barrier between the Jews, God's chosen people, and the rest of humanity was broken or broken down, Paul calls them Gentiles. The apostle Paul told the brethren of Ephesus that, "Christ is our peace. He made Jews and non-Jews one people, destroyed the wall that separated them, and annulled in his own body the hostility that existed. He put an end to the law consisting of mandates and regulations, and in himself created from the two parties a single new man. That's how he made peace. He put an end, in himself, to the hostility that existed between the two people, and with his death on the cross reconciled them to God, making them one body".[376]

With this Pauline declaration, the tearing of the veil in the Jewish Temple is a presentation of the union between the two people: Jews and Gentiles. That is to say that: "... after

[375] George H. Guthrie. *Comment with application: HEBREWS. From the biblical text to a contemporary application.* (Miami, Florida. Editorial Vida. 2014), 220.
[376] Ephesians 2:14'16, (DHH).

Christ's death, access to the Most Holy Place was widely open
(v. Hebrews 4:16), and its mysteries were so clear and revealed
that even the one who runs can clearly read the meaning they
contain".[377] The death of Jesus Christ on the cross cleanses us
from all sin, as the apostle John says, [378] but it also puts us in
a New Town. It puts us on a New Path.

And what does this mean? It means that it has an
ecclesiological significance. That is to say, "under the high
priesthood of Jesus, the people of God come to enjoy a new and
happy situation, and that is that now, believers - in Christ Jesus -
can constantly enter the presence of God, and they can do so
with 'firmness'."[379] the tearing of the veil indicates that there is
now a New Path to reach God; A New Path to walk with God
completely forgiven and free from our sins! The Veil was torn!

There is, then, a Path that, if we walk along it, we will
be completely transformed. Have you ever wondered why
some do not want to walk on this Path? Why do some hide
behind a torn veil? Most of them do it out of fear or fear of
being different.

1. In their fear, they cling to the past. This was the
   case with the Jews of the time of Jesus of Nazareth,
   they wanted to continue in their way of life; they did
   not want the change what Christ proposed to them.
   Today we have people boxed in, locked in their fears
   of change. Although they are not well emotionally,
   psychologically and less spiritually, they say, " I am
   good."

---

[377]   Matthew Henry. *Exegetical-Devotional Commentary on the Entire Bible: Matthew.*
         Td. Francisco Lacueva. (Terrassa (Barcelona), Spain. Editorial CLIE. 1984), 552.
[378]   I John 1:9.
[379]   George H. Guthrie. *Comment with application: HEBREWS. From the biblical text
         to a contemporary application.* (Miami, Florida. Editorial Vida. 2014), 220

2. Fear of what they will say. What are people going to say? If I go the New Path that God has made by tearing the veil; What are people going to say? That I betrayed my parents! That I betrayed my religion! That I betrayed my country! What are people going to say? I continue to die in my pain, in my anguish, in my grievances and in my fears instead of trying to walk the New Path that Jesus Christ opened.

3. Fear that they will discover my sins. The New Path that Jesus Christ inaugurated with his death and that the tearing of the veil approves it, is a Path of light, where everything can be seen; it is a Path in which day by day we are being transformed into the image of Christ. It is a Path to Holiness!

Did you know that fear is a very high barrier to happiness? If you didn't know, now you know. You can't be happy with a mind and heart cloistered by fear! Fear closes the door to happiness!

The light that this New Path contains, and the holiness it requires, makes us transparent; That is, everything we are and do is seen by God and His Holy Spirit will tell us the sin we are doing. The Bible says that: "... the Spirit examines everything, even the deepest things of God".[380]

We cannot hide from God! The veil is torn! There is no possibility of hiding from his presence. So why do some try to hide from God, even though that's impossible, but why do they try? I think one of the reasons why some don't want to walk the New Path is for fear of having their sins discovered.

Beloved brothers and sisters in Christ, friends, you who are listening to me, or reading this book, all your fears will

---

[380] I Corinthians 2:10, (DHH).

be waste, they will be taken away from you, little by little the Lord will transform you into a person of good and with the necessary peace you need as you walk along the New Path that was opened when the veil of the temple was torn from top to bottom.

The presentation of the tearing of the veil as a symbol of the union that God desires among humanity is an irrefutable fact. Remember that God, through the death of Christ Jesus, made one people; he put peace among human beings. A peace that offers you if you dare to walk along the New Path.

CONCLUSION.

The tearing of the veil presents the new way to draw closer to God. One day the Lord Jesus said that he was the Way, the truth and the life and that no one could reach the Father but only through him.[381] The tearing of the veil in the Jewish temple meant "the consecration and inauguration of a new path to God".[382]

That is to say that now the only thing that prevents you from having communion with God the Father is your decision. You decide to walk towards and with God or to continue walking in your own ways.

It's your decision! The door is already opened, and you don't have to make any sacrifices, not even open the Door, why? Because the Door is already opened! It is only to make the decision to enter the Path of God. I repeat, it's your decision!

---

[381] John 14:6. (Transliterated by Eleazar Barajas)

[382] Matthew Henry. *Exegetical-Devotional Commentary on the Entire Bible: Matthew.* Td. Francisco Lacueva. (Terrassa (Barcelona), Spain. Editorial CLIE. 1984), 552.

TREMOR WITH PURPOSE

"The earth trembled, the rocks were broken, and the tombs were opened; and even many holy people, who had died, came back to life. Then they came out of their tombs, after the resurrection of Jesus, and entered the holy city of Jerusalem, where many people saw them".
Matthew 27:51b-53, (DHH)

INTRODUCTION.

Nothing new to us, especially those of us who live in Southern California, tremors and or earthquakes are very familiar. They may not have a specific purpose, but they do frighten us and tell us that we have life "tied" by a thread that, at any moment, will be broken.

According to the journalist, Carlos Moreno: "The Veracruz Earthquake of 1973 or also known as The Orizaba Earthquake, has been the strongest earthquake that has taken place in Mexico, the second deadliest and the fourteenth strongest in history that has been recorded by unofficial data.

The earthquake arose during the early morning of Tuesday, August 28 at 4:52 a.m. with a duration of almost 3 minutes in the central area of Veracruz and with a magnitude of between 7.3 and up to 8.7 on the Richter scale (according to Veracruz seismograph), other reliable sources claim that the earthquake was 8.5".[383] This earthquake, in Cordoba, Veracruz, caused a hole in the back wall of the church.

The Evangelist Matthew speaks of a tremor that, the way he describes it, seems to have been an earthquake. At the same time, we noticed that the tremor of the Calvary was for clear purposes.

1.- ENFORCE MESSIANIC COMPLIANCE.

Notice that it was a local tremor with which interesting and miraculous things happened: The veil of the temple that was almost unbreakable, was torn from top to bottom. The rocks split, this indicates that it was not just a tremor, but an earthquake. Also: "The tombs were opened".[384] Well, this can happen with any other tremor, yet evangelist Matthew goes on to say that "many saints who had died were resurrected". And not only were they resurrected, but: "They came out of the tombs, and, after the resurrection of Jesus, they entered the holy city and appeared to many".[385]

These local events were miracles performed by God Himself to make people feel messianic fulfillment. At the same time, they were clear examples that the one who was crucified on the Calvary was the same God, whom nature respects and whimpers waiting for the last coming.

---

[383]   Carlos Moreno. *1973 earthquake of the city of Córdoba.* (La Habra, California. Internet. Article retrieved May 1, 2021), ¿http://cronicas.ugmex.edu.mx/index.php/ enterate/1132-temblor-de-1973-de-la-ciudad-de-cordoba

[384]   Matthew 27:52, (KJV, 1960).

[385]   Matthew 27:52-53, (NIV).

The apostle Paul says that: "... we know that the whole creation whimpers and suffers pains of childbirth until now".[386] From the context of Matthew, I believe that those present at the Calvary understood that the events were not a mere coincidence, but something directly from God. Matthew said that: "When the centurion and those who were guarding Jesus with him saw the earthquake and everything that had happened, they were terrified".[387] Being terrified is a very big fear or dread, an intense fear. It's like when someone says it's getting scary cold.

Very few people are frightened to the point of being terrified by a tremor, this tells us that it was a strong tremor that was announcing that the messianic fulfillment had reached Jerusalem.

II.- MAKE PEOPLE FEEL A LITTLE REMORSE THAT WOULD LEAD THEM TO REPENTANCE OF THEIR SINS.

God always seeks the means for people to recognize that there are things and events that only He can do. And when it does, it is to lead them to repent of their sins. In this case, we are seeing something extremely interesting and miraculous. I said that people were terrified; that the were very afraid and that some, among them, the Roman Centurion, recognized that Jesus was not just any human being, but was the promised Messiah, he, as a Roman, said referring to Jesus Christ: "This man was truly the Son of God!"[388]

---

386   Romans 8:22, (New Latin American Bible).
387   Matthew 27:54, (NIV).
388   Matthew 27:54b. (NTV).

Experts in Geology (Geo, γῆ, earth. Lodge λογία, study), say that: "Because of the geological characteristics of Palestine, which sits on a major seismic fault, an earthquake would not be something unusual, but if it is accompanied by rocks that break and tombs that open, then this is another relevant testimony of the meaning of the crucifixion of Jesus".[389] God does wonderful things in order to lead us to repentance! And in each of them it has a well-defined purpose.

It is interesting to note that although it was an earthquake that tore the veil and split the rocks, the cross did not fall! Let us remember that Matthew says that those who were at the foot of the cross-standing guard were terrified, this means that Mount Calvary trembled strongly, but the cross did not fall!

God was still in control! The worst events can happen, and God is still in control! There will always be a purpose in each of them and a sign that God is in control. The cross did not fall! The cross, with the crucified one carrying him, was saying that, in the midst of crises and fears, whatever the magnitude of them, if eyes are lifted up to Jesus Christ, sins and fears can be forgiven and annulled.

III.- TO NOTE THAT DEATH HAD BEEN DEFEATED.

The evangelist Matthew says that "many holy people, who had died, came back to life".[390] Interesting statement! Jesus Christ died to give life. When the apostle Paul speaks of

---

[389] Michael J. Wilkins. *Bible Commentary with Application: MATTHEW: From the Biblical Text to a Contemporary Application.* (Nashville, Tennessee, USA. Editorial Vida. 2016), 905

[390] Matthew 27:52, (DHH).

the resurrection of the dead, he asks, "Where is your victory, O death? Where is it, O death, your sting?" And then he gives the answer, saying that: "The sting of death is sin, and the power of sin is the law. But thank God, who gives us victory through our Lord Jesus Christ!"[391]

"The fear of death has always tormented people... - But where does the fear of death come from? Partly from the fear of the unknown. But even more, of the feeling of sin".[392] There is within us a constant feeling of guilt. It is a guilt caused by sin and it provokes the fear of death.

By keeping the cross in place amid the chaos caused by the earthquake, God assures that death has been overcome and with it the fear of death. "For that Jesus gave us the victory over death, banishing their fear with the wonder of God's love".[393]

Certainly, the tremor made it known that death had been overcome. But what else does it teach us?

1. *That nature itself was hurt by the death of Jesus Christ.* It could be said that nature wept with pain at seeing the Son of God die on such a cruel cross. But at the same time, it wept with happiness as his redemption was approaching.

2. *That nature itself testifies that there is a supreme being with extraordinary power over it.* Why do some talk about Mother Earth? Mother Earth and her equivalence as a Mother Goddess is a theme that appears in many mythologies. "Mother Earth is the

---

[391] I Corinthians 15:55-57, (NIV).

[392] William Barclay. *Comentario al Nuevo Testamento: 1 y 2 Corintios. Volume 9.* (Terrassa (Barcelona), España. Editorial CLIE. 1996), 194

[393] William Barclay. *Commentary on the New Testament: 1 and 2 Corinthians. Volumen 9.* (Terrassa (Barcelona), Spain. Editorial CLIE. 1996), 195

personification of the Earth, described in various cultures as a fertile goddess, ... The United Nations establishes April 22 as International Mother Earth Day".[394]

Since the Calvary, regardless of everything they say, nature affirms that there is a supernatural power over it. She affirms that a Supreme Being makes her break the rocks, makes her tear the veil, makes her rise to the dead, but forces her to keep the cross in place. There is a Supreme Being over nature!

3. *That nature itself testifies to how great and perverse the sin of humanity is.* That is to say: "That this earthquake means... The horrible wickedness of those who crucified Christ. Trembling under such a great weight, the earth bore witness to the innocence – of Jesus Christ, while testifying against – the ungodliness of the persecutors".[395] As if in a tone of anguish or tantrum against the sin of humanity, nature tore the veil, broke the rocks and opened the tombs, by the way, not all the deceased of the open tombs were resurrected, only the saints! Ah, wonders of God's power!

4. *That nature itself, in a very mysterious way, recognized that from that moment there would be a new era.* The law came to an end and grace took over. "This earthquake also means the blow dealt to Satan's kingdom".[396] A new era was beginning! God's

---

[394]   Madre Tierra. *Simbología del mundo.* (La Habra, California. Internet. Consultado el 1 de mayo del 2021) ¿? https://simbologiadelmundo.com/madre-tierra/

[395]   Mathew Henry. *Comentario Exegético-Devocional a toda la Biblia: Mateo. Td. Francisco* Lacueva. (Terrassa (Barcelona), España. Editorial CLIE. 1984), 552.

[396]   Mathew Henry. *Exegetical-Devotional Commentary on the Entire Bible: Matthew.* Td. Francisco Lacueva. (Terrassa (Barcelona), Spain. Editorial CLIE. 1984), 552.

love overcame the terrifying designs of the satanic kingdom.

5.   *That nature itself announces that at the last trumpet the earth will be removed,* while it teaches that no one knows when it will happen. No one expected an earthquake at three o'clock on the Calvary.

CONCLUSION.

God, with the earthquake of the Calvary, made the messianic fulfillment felt. God fulfilled His Word! In His passion for seeing people with a new vision and a new heart, God made people feel a little remorse that led them to repentance for their sins. Moreover, God, through the earthquake, noted that death had been overcome.

What else do you need to believe in God? What other miracle do you want to see to believe that Jesus Christ is the last and only solution to your sins?

God willing a spiritual earthquake would shake you so you can see Jesus Christ dying for your sins.

TRULY: THERE IS NO DOUBT!

"The Roman officer and the other soldiers who were
at the crucifixion were terrified by the earthquake
and by everything that had happened. They said,
'This man was truly the Son of God!'."
Matthew 27:54, (NIV).

INTRODUCTION.

Surely you saw on social networks the video of when a young lady tells her mother – she does not ask for permission, she only tells her – that she is going with some friends to a picnic.

The worried mother says, "Daughter, may God be with you". "Well, if it fits in the trunk, it's fine, because inside we are already tight" – was the response of the young lady.

On the road they had a terrible accident. They all died. When one of the traffic officers opened the trunk, he was surprised to see that the eggs they were carrying to eat at the camp were intact in the basket where they had been laid. He said to himself. "This can't be".[397]

---

[397]   YouTube. *DON'T UNDERESTIMATE GOD, NO ONE MOCKS GOD!!!* (La Habra, California. Internet: YouTube. Retrieved March 12, 2021), ¿? https://www.youtube.com/watch?v=Qeq8MavOuiE

That young lady and her companions did not have time to make sure that the One who was in the trunk: "Truly was the Son of God".[398]

Pastor, are there more surprises that make us exclaim and assure that Jesus Christ *truly was the Son of God*? Yes, there are more surprises! Let's think about some of them.

I.- THE SURPRISE OF A VICARIOUS DEATH.

In the last minutes of Jesus' life on the Cross in that Last Week of His earthly ministry, the earth testified about Who was dying on that Cross on Mount Calvary and, therefore, shuddered. He moved with such force as showing his pain that those who were the proud soldiers were *terrified by the earthquake and by everything that had happened.* After going through an experience of that magnitude, they recognize who was the One they had crucified and announced it as a testimony so that humanity recognizes that Jesus Nazarene WAS and IS a human being who suffered all the pains equal to or worse than another human being. In the midst of that unpleasant experience, they testified, *Truly this is the Son of God.*

"When theologians later reflected on the words spoken by Jesus from the cross, they recognized that, at the time... From his death, he suffered the punishment of mankind for sin, namely death".[399] I remind you once again of what the apostle Paul has said about Jesus' agony on the Calvary, Paul said, "For the wages of sin is death, but the gift that God gives

---

398   Matthew 27:54c, (NIV).
399   Michael J Wilkins. *Bible Commentary with Application: MATTHEW: From the Biblical Text to a Contemporary Application.* (Nashville, Tennessee, USA. Editorial Vida. 2016), 918.

is eternal life through Christ Jesus our Lord".[400] The depth of this text can be understood: "Only by recalling the bleak aspect of life outside of Christ – in that kind of life – can we truly appreciate the magnitude of God's 'gift,' the gift of his Grace that imparts 'eternal life in Christ Jesus our Lord'."[401] Although it was already written in the Holy Scriptures of the Old Testament, no one imagined that Jesus would be the vicar of God! Even the same Satan who attacked him so much from his childhood until that day was on the Cross, the surprise of vicarious death surely terrified him, because he realized that he had lost the final battle

II.- THE SURPRISE OF THE MAGNET OF THE CROSS.

I understand that we all know magnets, although not everyone knows how they work in their action of attracting: "A natural magnet is a bar, usually straight or horseshoe-shaped, that has two distinct poles, the positive pole and the negative pole (or also known as North and South)".[402] The Bible says that there is salvation effected and guaranteed by Jesus Christ; but there is also God's judgment for everyone who rejects salvation. That is, Salvation and Condemnation are two opposites: Positive and Negative, (*North and South*).

The function of the magnet is to attract. But how does it do it? "When we bring a magnet closer to another magnet at one end, it can happen that these are attracted or repelled,

---

[400] Romans 6:23, (NLT).

[401] Douglas J. Moo. *Romans: Commentary with application; from the biblical text to a contemporary application.* (Miami, Florida. Editorial Vida. 2011), 205

[402] A. Ball. How a magnet works. (La Habra, California. Internet. Retrieved September 22, 2021), ¿? http://comofunciona.org/como-funciona-un-iman/

depending on whether we bring them closer to a positive pole with a negative pole (they attract), a negative pole with a negative pole (they repel) or a positive pole with a positive pole (they repel)".[403] Interesting action of the magnet. Now, what does this have to do with the surprise of the magnetism of the cross? God or Jesus Christ will always be positive (Positive Pole) and humanity has always been negative (Negative Pole). And here is the great blessing for humanity; on the Cross, Jesus Christ attracted, first, all kinds of sin to be forgiven.

The scene we can see from the biblical account is that Jesus was hanging from the Cross and the soldiers at the foot of it watching the crucified one. After the darkness and the earthquake that frightened them, the Roman centurion exclaimed saying that Jesus was truly a righteous or innocent man.[404]

Now, how do we relate the fact that Jesus was innocent or just and at the same time sinner or cursed for carrying our sins upon his person? The apostle Paul told the Galatians, "Christ rescued us from the curse of the law by making himself a curse for our sake, for Scripture says, 'Cursed is he who dies hanging on a tree'."[405] The apostle Peter said: "He – Jesus Christ – himself, in his body, bore our sins to the wood, that we may die to sin and live for righteousness. By your wounds you have been healed".[406] Once again the apostle Paul says, "He who committed no sin for us was treated as a sinner by God, so that in him we might receive the righteousness of God".[407]

---

[403]   A. Ball. *How a magnet works*. (La Habra, California. Internet. Retrieved September 22, 2021), ¿? http://comofunciona.org/como-funciona-un-iman/

[404]   Luke 23:47.

[405]   Galatians 3:13, (DHH).

[406]   I Peter 2:24, (NIV).

[407]   2 Corinthians 5:21, (NIV).

So, then, if Jesus bore the sin of mankind and if he became *cursed* and if *God treated him as a sinner,* was Jesus' innocent when he was on the cross or was, he a sinner whom God the Father did not want to see because of His Sin? Benny Hinn, in one of his messages said: "He [Jesus] who is righteous by choice said, 'The only way I can stop sin is to become it. I can't help it, letting it touch me, I and it must be one. Listen to this! He who is of the nature of God has become of the nature of Satan when he became sin!'."[408] Nathan Busenitz says that: "Copeland reiterates that same teaching – saying, 'How did Jesus then on the cross say, 'My God'? Because God was not His father anymore. He took upon Himself the nature of Satan'."[409]

On the other side of the coin, we find that, the prophet Isaiah spoken of the ministry of Jesus Christ, said that: "We were all lost, like sheep; each one followed his own way, but the Lord made the iniquity of us all fall upon him".[410] The apostle John told his contemporaries, "And you know that he – Christ Jesus – appeared to take away our sins, and there is no sin in him".[411]

These biblical texts (and others like Luke 23:47; Romans 5:19; Philippians 2:8; and Hebrews 4:15, where it says, "For we have not a high priest who cannot sympathize with our weaknesses, but one who has been tempted in everything as

---

[408] Nathan Busenitz. *Did Jesus Become a Sinner on the Cross?* (Benny Hinn, Trinity Broadcasting Network, December 1, 1990). (La Habra, California. Internet. Retrieved September 22, 2021), ¿? https://evangelio.blog/2013/11/21/jess-se-hizo-pecador-en-la-cruz/

[409] Nathan Busenitz. *Did Jesus Become a Sinner on the Cross?* (Kenneth Copeland, "Believer's Voice of Victory," Trinity Broadcasting Network, April 21, 1991). (La Habra, California. Internet. Retrieved September 22, 2021), ¿? https://evangelio.blog/2013/11/21/jess-se-hizo-pecador-en-la-cruz/

[410] Isaiah 53:6, (NIV). Underlining and *italics* are mine.

[411] I John 3:5, (KJV, 1960). The **Bold** and the *Italics* are mine.

we are, **but without sin**".[412] (The Bold and underlined are mine), all these texts claim that Jesus was sinless. How, then, do we explain the apparent contrast of statements? Was Jesus a sinner on the Cross or was He innocent? "The best way to understand Paul's statement (that Jesus became sin for us) is in terms of imputation. Our sin was imputed to Christ, so that it became a substitutionary sacrifice or atonement for all who believed in Him".[413] That is, Jesus, in his forgiving positivism, attracted, like the magnet, all kinds of sin and the same original sin to Him while still being the righteous one. The magnet does not become what it attracts.

Second, Jesus, on the Cross, not only attracted sin to deliver us from it, but also provided salvation; that is, Jesus "pulls" every human being who approaches him and takes away his sin. Again, we say that although Jesus draws sinners to himself, Jesus does not become them: He is still God the Savior! The magnet attracts without becoming what it attracts.

After a terrifying experience, there on the cusp of the Calvary, the scene is transformed into something hopeful. "Jesus' death vividly impressed the centurion and the multitude. His death had the effect it had not had on his life: breaking the hard human's heart. What Jesus was saying was already being fulfilled: 'When I am raised from the earth, I will draw all men to Me'. (John 12:32). The magnet of the cross had begun to take effect at the very moment of Jesus' death".[414] Amen!!

---

[412]   I John 3:5, (KJV, 1960). The **Bold** and the *Italics* are mine.

[413]   Nathan Busenitz. *Did Jesus Become a Sinner on the Cross?* (Benny Hinn, Trinity Broadcasting Network, December 1, 1990 (La Habra, California. Internet. Retrieved September 22, 2021), ¿? https://evangelio.blog/2013/11/21/jess-se-hizo-pecador-en-la-cruz/

[414]   William Barclay. *Commentary on the New Testament: Volume 4: LUKE.* (Terrassa (Barcelona), Spain. Editorial CLIE. 1994), 346.

III.- THE SURPRISE OF THE EVENTS NEAR THE CROSS.

Nothing like it! In Buddha's case, "his closest disciples were perplexed as they tried to understand what his nature was. They asked, 'Lord, after death, does the Tathágata exist, does it not exist, both cases or neither?' and he always offered the same answer: 'It is not pertinent to say that a Buddha exists after death. It is not appropriate to say that a Buddha does not exist after death. Neither is it to say that a Buddha, both, exists (in one sense) as it does not exist (in another) after death. It is not appropriate to say that a Buddha neither exists nor does not exist after death. Any way of explaining or describing the issue is inappropriate'."[415] What are we left with? Who knows what! Because the Tathāgata or Tathagata attributes Gautama Buddha himself to refer to himself. "It is translated as 'he who has thus come' (Thatā - āgata) or 'he who has thus gone' (Thatā - cat). It has also been pointed out as a translation of this term: *'he who has attained the truth'.*[416] Does he finally die, or does he not die? And, if he dies, what is achieved by his death? Apparently, nothing certain! Then, the death of Buddha left uncertainty.

On Muhammad's death it is said that: "In the last two years of Muhammad's life Islam spread to the rest of Arabia. When Muhammad died without a male heir, disputes broke out over the succession, which fell to the prophet's son-in-law, Abu Bakr, thus becoming the first caliph or successor".[417] Muhammad's death left "disputes".

---

[415] *Buddhist texts and books. Reflections on death.* (La Habra, California. Internet. Retrieved September 22, 2021), https://www.budismo-valencia.com/budismo/muerte-buda

[416] Wikipedia, the free encyclopedia. *Tathāgata.* (La Habra, California. Internet. Retrieved September 22, 2021), ¿? https://es.wikipedia.org/wiki/Tath%C4%81gata

[417] Great Encyclopedia Rialp. *Brief biography of Muhammad.* (La Habra, California. Internet. Retrieved September 22, 2021), ¿? https://www.gecoas.com/religion/historia/medieval/EM-A.htm

In Mexico, the deaths of Don Miguel Hidalgo y Costilla, the priest Don José María Morelos y Pavón and all the others considered the heroes of Mexican Independence, left a country completely divided, with an inconsistent policy and with well-marked traces of a slavery that is still practiced.

The Biblical Story of *The Last Week* of The Life of Jesus Christ on This Earth presents us with the surprise of the events near the Cross. Part of this story says that: "... the centurion – a Roman who stood next to the Cross of Jesus – and his men saw Jesus die and - heard his great cries, especially the last one, when Jesus cried out: 'Father, in your hands I commend my spirit' -... As they watched the supernatural darkening of the sky, the veil of the temple torn in two, the earthquake, and how the tombs were opened, they suddenly realized that Jesus might be who he claimed to be. And, utterly overwhelmed, they uttered, 'Truly this was the Son of God!' (Matt.27:54)".[418] They were surprised by God Himself!

The death of Jesus on the Cross of the Calvary, in addition to the surprises we have noticed, also ensured an eternal freedom from all sin; a freedom from evil and a freedom from satanic power itself.

CONCLUSION.

One of the great promises we have in the Bible is the Second Coming of Jesus Christ. Many hundreds of years have passed since Jesus Christ said, "I am the way, the truth, and the life. Only by me can the Father be reached. ... And if I go

---

[418]   Michael J Wilkins. *Bible Commentary with Application: MATTHEW: From the Biblical Text to a Contemporary Application.* (Nashville, Tennessee, USA. Editorial Vida. 2016), 920-921.

and prepare a place for you, I will come again and take you with me; that where I am, there you may also be".[419] .

The apostles were convinced of Jesus' return to earth in bodily form. Paul said, "The Lord Himself will descend from heaven with the voice of command, with the voice of an archangel, and with the trumpet of God".[420] The apostle Peter said, "The Lord does not take long to fulfill his promise, as some understand the tardiness. Rather, he has patience with you, because he does not want anyone to perish, but everyone to repent. But the day of the Lord will come like a thief. On that day the heavens will disappear with a dreadful rumble, the elements will be destroyed by fire, and the earth, with all that is in it, will be burned".[421] In the Book of Revelation, the Glorified Christ said to John, "He who declares this", that is, everything revealed to John in Revelation, says, 'Yes, I am coming soon'. And John's answer was: Amen. Come, Lord Jesus!"[422]

Truly: There is no doubt! Jesus Christ will return a second time to this earth in a bodily way. Every eye will see you! says the Scripture. My question is: Will you be surprised by his coming? Will you be surprised like the policeman who saw the basket of eggs without any of them being broken in that car accident? Will you be surprised how he surprised those at the foot of the Cross?

I hope you are not surprised by the Second Coming of Jesus Christ. Remember: Truly: There is no doubt! Jesus Christ will return a second time to this earth in a bodily way.

Wait for it!

Amen!

---

[419] John 14:6, (DHH); John 14:3, (The Bible of the Americas).
[420] I Thessalonians 4:14, (NIV).
[421] 2 Peter 3:9-10, (NIV).
[422] Revelation 22:20, (DHH).

THE OTHER TEAM

"They were there, looking from afar, many women who had followed Jesus from Galilee to serve him. Among them were Mary Magdalene, Mary the mother of James and Joseph, and the mother of the children of Zebedee".
Matthew 27:55-56, (NIV).

INTRODUCTION.

The evangelist Matthew speaks of "*Many women*" who were on Mount Calvary while Jesus was crucified. He mentions three of them by name and emphasizes that two of them were mothers: Mary Magdalene, Mary the mother of James and Joseph, and the mother of Zebedee's children.

Jesus died. According to Matthew's account, a strong earthquake frightened those who were caring for the crucified. I imagine some ran downhill. Right there was *The Other Team* of the Lord Jesus. Matthew calls him, "*Many women.*" By the way, the *First Team* called the Apostolic Body, except for John, was hidden. It was a Team that, now Jesus needed, and they abandoned him for fear of the authorities.

Now, during all that chaos of darkness, of a strong earthquake, of split rocks, of open tombs, what was this Other Team doing?

I.- THEY WERE OBSERVING.

The evangelist Matthew says that the *Other Team*: "They were there, looking from afar",[423] There they were looking from afar, "since at that time they could not render any service to him, they directed at least a look of affection, a look of sorrow",[424] a look of pain, a pain so deep from the bottom of their souls for seeing Jesus in those circumstances. Why from afar? *First,* because they were Jewish women and those who were taking care of the crucified were Romans. There was no friendship between the Jews and the Romans. So, this Other Team couldn't get close to the crucified one because it had a cultural barrier in between. However, he was ready to act at the time he was asked.

Second, Jewish women were subjected to a misinterpretation of Jewish law. From the beginning, when God created the human being, He did it to complement each other. "Women and men were originally created by God as equals and as collaborators who complemented each other to rule the divine creation in His name (Gen. 1:26-28)".[425] Over time, this biblical truth was distorted and a misinterpretation of Jewish law left women without dignity, worthlessness and without any merit.

---

[423]   Matthew 27:55, (NIV).
[424]   Matthew Henry. *Exegetical-Devotional Commentary on the Entire Bible: Matthew.* Td. Francisco Lacueva. (Terrassa (Barcelona), Spain. Editorial CLIE. 1984), 555-556.
[425]   Michael J. Wilkins. *Bible Commentary with Application: MATTHEW: From the Biblical Text to a Contemporary Application.* (Nashville, Tennessee, USA. Editorial Vida. 2016), 921.

The Jewish historian Josephus said that: "According to the law, woman is in everything inferior to man".[426] Big mistake! The fact that they are watching on the Calvary does not mean that they are inferior, but that they are in the best disposition to serve Jesus Christ even in the worst circumstances. Where was the First Team? Hidden somewhere. In this scene, far from being inferior, women show a higher value than men. There they were, watching, knowing that they could be arrested.

There they were watching everything that was happening as if to say, how can we help Him? "It has been said that, unlike men, women had nothing to fear, because their public position was so unreported that no one would notice female disciples".[427] Maybe that was true. But we cannot deny the courage and love they showed by standing there in front of the crucified. "They were there because they loved Jesus; and for them, as for so many others, perfect love casts out fear".[428]

Third, Jewish women were marginalized by a prayer that some Jewish rabbis invented and that accelerated the idea that women have no dignity, no value, and no merit. That prayer says, "Praise be to God for not making me a Gentile! Praise be to God for not having created me a woman! Praise be to God who has not created me ignorant!"[429]

Ah, vain thoughts of men who don't realize that racism and discrimination is part of ignorance! Ah, vain thoughts

[426] Michael J. Wilkins. *Bible Commentary with Application: MATTHEW: From the Biblical Text to a Contemporary Application.* (Nashville, Tennessee, USA. Editorial Vida. 2016), 921.

[427] William Barclay. *Commentary on the New Testament: Volume 2: MATTHEW: II.* Trd. Alberto Araujo. (Terrassa (Barcelona), Spain. Editorial CLIE. 1997), 428.

[428] William Barclay. *Commentary on the New Testament: Volume 2: MATTHEW: II.* Trd. Alberto Araujo. (Terrassa (Barcelona), Spain. Editorial CLIE. 1997), 428.

[429] Michael J. Wilkins. *Bible Commentary with Application: MATTHEW: From the Biblical Text to a Contemporary Application.* (Nashville, Tennessee, USA. Editorial Vida. 2016), 921.

that prevent them from seeing that a woman's love overcomes any barrier! There they were watching to see where they would be useful.

II.- THEY WERE STANDING.

These women had followed Jesus from Galilee to the Calvary itself for one purpose only: to serve Him! So, we're talking about these being remarkable women. Its merits can be seen in at least two admirable actions:

1. "They showed a value that is difficult to find.
2. They had given evidence of having hearts full of love and understanding".[430]

Dignity, courage, merit, equality and respect for women is what Jesus Christ highlighted in each of the ladies who accompanied him during his earthly ministry. That is, "A direct result of Jesus' ministry was the restoration and affirmation of women".[431] This is a fact we note in the gospels. They, the Other Team, who stood in front of the crucified one, in the same spirit of service, were given the following five credits by the four evangelists:

1. "Women are equally deserving of the saving activity of Jesus (John 4:1-42).

---

[430]   William Hendriksen. *The Gospel of Matthew: Commentary on the New Testament.* (Grand Rapids, Michigan. Distributed by T.E.L.L. Subcommittee On Christian Literature. 1986), 1026.

[431]   Michael J. Wilkins. *Bible Commentary with Application: MATTHEW: From the Biblical Text to a Contemporary Application.* (Nashville, Tennessee, USA. Editorial Vida. 2016), 921.

2. Women were called to be disciples of Jesus (Matthew 12:48-50).
3. Women received instruction and education as disciples of Jesus (Luke 10:38-42).
4. Women are part of the ministerial team (Luke 8:1-3).
5. By their courageous presence at the cross and in the tomb, women were appointed to be the first to bear witness to the resurrection of Jesus (Matthew 28:10; Mark 16:7; John 20:17)".[432]

Always ready to serve! It was not the custom for a rabbi to have a woman as his disciple, but Jesus did. Jesus not only saw the love that you women have for the Kingdom of God, but He also saw the potential that you have. A potential that makes the Lord's Church stand out in any circumstance.

Go ahead, women, God has called you to be mothers not only of your biological children but also of your spiritual children! Both need help with that potential for service that God has endowed them with.

III.- THEY WERE SEATED.

After the soldiers finished their task, it was time to bury Jesus' body. "The group that attended the funeral was small and insignificant: in addition to Joseph – of Arimathea – Mary Magdalene and the other Mary... The same ones who were present at the Calvary also followed him to the tomb".[433]

---

[432] Michael J. Wilkins. *Bible Commentary with Application: MATTHEW: From the Biblical Text to a Contemporary Application.* (Nashville, Tennessee, USA. Editorial Vida. 2016), 921-922.

[433] Matthew Henry. *Exegetical-Devotional Commentary on the Entire Bible: Matthew.* Td. Francisco Lacueva. (Terrassa (Barcelona), Spain. Editorial CLIE. 1984), 558.

What fidelity! The courage and tenacity of these women is admirable.

His example teaches us that: "True love for Christ will not allow us to leave him to the end".[434] In the sixth Song of songs, the beloved says to the beloved: "Record me as a seal upon your heart; take me as a mark on your arm. Strong is love, like death, ... As a divine flame is the burning fire of love. Neither the many waters can extinguish it, nor the rivers can extinguish it".[435] This kind of love is what the women of the Other Team showed.

Well, the time of the Sabbath was very close, so they hurried to bury him. The burial was so fast that there was no time to make all the corresponding preparations for the burial. The Bible says that: "At dusk, a rich man from Arimathea, named Joseph, ... took the body, wrapped it in a clean sheet, and put it in a new tomb...and left. There they were, *sitting in front of the tomb*, Mary Magdalene and the other Mary".[436]

Notice that two of the women of the *Other Team* sat in front of the tomb. Another version says, *"They continued there"*.[437] Another version is more emphatic, because it says that they were: *"There sitting in front of the tomb"*.[438] What faithfulness of these women! Apparently, they stayed there all night, In the morning Pilate's guard arrived to continue with the care of the tomb.

Beautiful and admirable Team! While some were tending the tomb, others, as soon as the day of rest was over, they

---

[434]   Matthew Henry. *Exegetical-Devotional Commentary on the Entire Bible: Matthew.* Td. Francisco Lacueva. (Terrassa (Barcelona), Spain. Editorial CLIE. 1984), 558.

[435]   Song of Songs 8:6-7, (NIV).

[436]   Matthew 27:57-61, (NIV). The italics are mine.

[437]   Bible Translation Committee. *New World Translation of the Holy Scriptures.* (New, York. USED. Watch Tower Bible and Tract Society of Pennsylvania e International Bible Students Association of Brooklyn, New York. 1961), 1987.

[438]   *Peshito Bible in Spanish.* (Nashville, Tennessee. Published by Holman Bible Publishers. 2000), 1076

went to buy and prepare the ointments that were used in the burials. "Saturday ended at sunset... They did not have time to do so when Jesus was buried, for the Sabbath was about to begin".[439]

So: "On Saturday evening, when the day of rest was over, Mary Magdalene, Salome, and Mary, the mother of James, went to buy spices for the burial, in order to anoint the body of Jesus. On Sunday morning very early, right at dawn, they went to the grave".[440]

Did you notice? When it was getting dark, they went out to buy the species for the burial and very early in the morning they were already on their way to the Cemetery. Ah, blessed were these tireless women! Blessed are these women who, when they have a commitment, draw strength from anywhere! Blessed are these women who with admirable courage served Jesus even in the worst circumstances! Blessed are these women who, even when seated, are serving the Lord!

Women, God bless you!

CONCLUSION.

The women who traveled with Jesus, that is, the *Other Team*, were of great help to the Lord. You women, God has given you the blessing of using the two parts of the brain, men use only one side, the left one that is associated with logical and rational thinking. *The First Team* used logic and rationality and that's why they hid.

Instead, you women, by using the logical, the rational, the affective, the intuition, and the imagination, whether you are

---

[439] Footnote in *the Schematic Study Bible.* (Brazil. United Bible Societies. 2010), 1481
[440] Mark 16:1, (NLT).

at a distance from necessity, whether you are on your feet or sitting, your potential for service is active.

Women, God has redeemed you, given you courage, given you dignity, given you merit, and empowered you with the potential to love and serve: Use that potential for the glory of God!

Amen!!!

THE TRUE ESSENCE OF CHRISTIANITY

- The Resurrection -

"Now, if it is preached that Christ has been raised
from the dead, how do some of you say that there
is no resurrection? If there is no resurrection, then
not even Christ is risen. And, if Christ is not risen,
our preaching is useless, nor is your faith".
I Corinthians 15:12-14, (NIV).

INTRODUCTION.

On one of the many missionary journeys Jesus made he went
to the city of Jerusalem. And: "As Jesus went up to Jerusalem,
he took the twelve disciples apart and said to them, 'Now we are
going to Jerusalem, and the Son of man will be handed over to the
chief priests and teachers of the law. They will condemn him to
death and deliver him to the Gentiles to mock him, scourge him,
and crucify him. But on the third day he will be resurrected'."[441]

---

[441]   Matthew 20:17-19, (NLT).

For the apostle Paul, the Resurrection of Jesus was and is something very essential in the New Age that Jesus Christ had initiated. Because, according to Paul: "If there is no resurrection, then not even Christ is risen. And, if Christ is not risen, our preaching is useless, so is your faith".[442] "Luther said that the doctrine of justification by faith was the doctrine of the church that was to remain or fall, but since Jesus Christ was raised up for our justification it would be more accurate to say that the doctrine of the church that was to remain or fall is that of the resurrection of the dead".[443] For John MacArthur: "The Resurrection of Jesus is the most important event in the history of the Redemption".[444] And then he adds: "The resurrection is not just a feature of Christianity, it is its essential truth. The point of the whole gospel is to rescue people from hell".[445]

So, then, if the true essence of Christianity is the Resurrection of Jesus, then, pastor, what lies in its essential truth? In response, I invite you to think about three essential truths of Jesus' Resurrection.

I.- JESUS, IN PROPHETIC FULFILLMENT, HAD TO DIE, BE BURIED AND BE RESURRECTED.

In a previous message I quoted the texts of Deuteronomy 21:22-23. "In this passage Moses ... emphasizes the law that

---

[442]　I Corinthians 15:13-14, (NIV).

[443]　Carroll, B. H. *Bible Commentary: James, Wrath and 2ⁿᵈ Thessalonians, 1ˢᵗ and 2ⁿᵈ Corinthians. Volume 10*. Trd. Sara A. Hale. (Terrassa (Barcelona), Spain. Editorial CLIE. 1987), 265.

[444]　John MacArthur. *The Resurrection of Jesus: The Most Important Event in the History of the Redemption*. (City of Commerce, California. Fuerza Latina Entertainment Inc. April 2014), 18.

[445]　John MacArthur. *The Resurrection of Jesus: The Most Important Event in the History of the Redemption*. (City of Commerce, California. Fuerza Latina Entertainment Inc. April 2014), 18.

commands the burial before sunset of the body of someone who has been sentenced to death and hanged from a stake (Mt 27:57-58; Jn19:31".[446] In the New Testament, we read that the apostle Paul said to the brethren of Rome, "Now, if we have died with Christ, we trust that we will also live with him. For we know that Christ, having been raised from the dead, can no longer die; death no longer has dominion over him. As for his death, he died to sin once and for all; as for his life, he lives for God".[447] Then, Jesus' resurrection fulfilled Bible prophecy.

So now, we ask ourselves the question: Did Jesus rise again? In 1907, a pastor was invited to preach at the Southern Baptist Convention meeting. In his preaching he said: "The body of Christ's resurrection was assumed on an interim basis, for the sole purpose of identification, and then it was eliminated. What did he do? We don't know, and it's not important that we know".[448] Seriously? Isn't it important that we know? We are talking about the resurrection of Jesus and, if it is not important that we know the whereabouts of Jesus' body, we are saying that the Resurrection of Jesus Christ is not essential to Christianity.

So, we ask ourselves again: Did Jesus rise again? The Lord had resurrected a young woman, the daughter of a man named Jairus. Jesus came to Jairus' house: "And taking the hand of the girl, he says to her, *Talita cumi*; which is, if you interpret it: Girl, to you I say, get up. Instantly the girl got up and started walking, she was twelve years old".[449] He also resurrected Lazarus of Bethany.[450]

---

[446]   Footnote in *the Schematic Study Bible*. (Brazil. United Bible Societies. 2010), 291.

[447]   Romans 6:8-10, (NVI).

[448]   Carroll, B. H. *Bible Commentary: James, Wrath and 2nd Thessalonians, 1st and 2nd Corinthians. Volume 10*. Trd. Sara A. Hale. (Terrassa (Barcelona), Spain. Editorial CLIE. 1987), 270.

[449]   Marcos 5:41-42 Biblia Jubileo 2000.

[450]   John 11:38-44.

A living person resurrecting a dead person may have some logic, but for a dead person to resurrect himself is something else. Although I will later show that Jesus did not rise alone, we still must return to the question: Did Jesus really rise on the third day of death?

Dr. B.H. Carroll presents in one of his books eleven facts that prove the resurrection of Jesus. He asks, "Did Jesus actually die, or would it just be a case of fainting, rapture, or other kind of suspenseful animation from which he subsequently recovered?"[451] And then he presents his eleven facts that prove that Jesus really rose again. It begins by saying that Jesus did die. In the seventh fact he mentions that a Roman guard was placed at the entrance of the tomb to take care that no one entered it and, in addition, in the sixth fact it says that a large stone was placed at the entrance of the tomb.[452] Fact that narrates the Gospel of Matthew in this way: "... The next day, after the day of preparation, the chief priests and Pharisees appeared before Pilate. Lord, they said, we remember that while that deceiver was still alive, he said, three days later He will be resurrected. Therefore, order that the tomb be sealed until the third day, we wouldn't want his disciples to come, steal the body and tell the people that He has risen. That last deception would be worse than the first. Take a few guards from the soldiers, Pilate ordered them, and go and secure the tomb as best you can. So they went, closed the tomb with a stone, and sealed it; and they kept guard".[453]

Neither the stone nor the Roman guard prevented Jesus from rising. On the third day, according to the prophecy that

---

[451] B. H. Carroll. *Bible Commentary: The Four Gospels. Volume 6. Volume II.* Trd. Sara A. Hale. (Terrassa (Barcelona), Spain. Editorial CLIE. 1986),475.

[452] B. H. Carroll. *Bible Commentary: The Four Gospels. Volume 6. Volume II.* Trd. Sara A. Hale. (Terrassa (Barcelona), Spain. Editorial CLIE. 1986),475-479.

[453] Mateo 27:62-66, (NIV).

Jesus himself had announced, a strong earthquake shook the place where Jesus' body was; an angel arrived, removed the stone, leaving the entrance free to the tomb and the guards were paralyzed by the fear or terror they felt when they saw what was happening around them. And who wouldn't be frightened by a "great earthquake" and seeing an angel sitting on the stone?

When the women arrived at the tomb, the angel, who was sitting on the removed stone, said to them: "...Do not be afraid. I know you are looking for Jesus, the one who was crucified. He is not here, but he is risen, he said. Come and see the place where they put him. Go and say to the disciples, 'He is risen, and he goes to Galilee to gather them again; there you will see Him'."[454] Jesus had to be resurrected to fulfill the Scriptures! Jesus had to be resurrected because this event is something essential to Christianity! Peter's words, filled with the Holy Spirit, when the members of the Sanhedrin asked them with what power and in the name of whom they had healed a lame,[455] he responded by saying, "Rulers and elders of our people, do you question us today for having done a good deed to a cripple? Do you want to know how you were healed? Let me say clearly to both you and all the people of Israel that they were healed by the mighty name of Jesus Christ of Nazareth, the man whom you crucified, *but whom God raised from the dead*".[456] Jesus Christ is not dead! Jesus Christ is not crucified! Jesus Christ is not in a tomb! He is risen!

Yes, the Lord is Risen! Repeat with me: The Lord is Risen! Jesus, in a prophetic fulfillment, had to die, be buried, and be resurrected. This is essential for every Christian because in

---

[454]   Matthew 28:5-7, (DHH); Luke 24:1-10.
[455]   Acts 4:8-10, (NLT).
[456]   Acts 3:1-10. The **bolds** and *italics* are mine.

this way it had been prophesied and thus, a great battle was won against sin, death and against the prince of this world himself, Satan.

Well, what happened to the soldiers who were guarding the entrance to the tomb where Jesus' body was? With them came two events that the Scriptures emphasize. First: They didn't lie. Thank God they didn't, otherwise we would have another fact to investigate, their lies. They told the truth. "They warned the chief priests – the so-called Sanhedrin – of all the things that had happened".[457]

Second: They were bribed. "A bribe is money, a favor, or other consideration given in exchange for someone's influence against what is true, right, or just. The Bible makes it clear that giving or receiving a bribe is a perverse thing".[458] The Evangelist Matthew says that the leaders of the Jews, i.e., The Sanhedrin, who were the Supreme Court among Judaism, "... They gave a lot of money to the soldiers, to whom they warned: You say that during the night, while you were sleeping, the disciples of Jesus came and stole the body. And if the governor finds out about this, we will convince him, and we will save you difficulties. The soldiers received the money and did as they had been told. And this is the explanation that to this day circulates among the Jews".[459]

And this is an explanation that to this day we notice, and we know what happens among our contemporary people. However: "When we try to deny such obvious realities as this – the Resurrection of Jesus of Nazareth – we end up highlighting the very reality we are trying to deny. It is

---

457   Matthew 28:11b, (KJV, 1960).
458   Got Questions. *What does the Bible say about bribery/giving or receiving a bribe?* (La Habra, California. Internet. Retrieved September 15, 2021), ¿? https://www.gotquestions.org/Espanol/biblia-soborno.html
459   Mateo 28:12b-15, (DHH).

inevitable, 'for we can do nothing against the truth, but by the truth' (2 Corinthians 13:8)".[460]

The incompressible, although still a Biblical-theological truth, is that, in the Resurrection of Jesus, the Holy Trinity plays a very important role. This gives more essential character to this event. The Bible says that...

1. *God raised Jesus from the dead.* The Bible says that: "... knowing that you were rescued from your vein way of living -by -, the precious blood of Christ, ... already destined since before the foundation of the world, ... and by which you believe in God, who raised him from the dead and gave him glory, that your faith and hope may be in God".[461]

It also says that: "The God who gives peace raised from the dead the great Shepherd of the sheep, our Lord Jesus, by the blood of the eternal covenant".[462] And Peter said, "... you killed Jesus, nailing him to the cross. However, God raised him, freeing him from the anguish of death, because it was impossible for death to keep him under His dominion".[463]

2. *That the Holy Spirit was the one who raised Jesus.* In Scripture we find this statement: "But if the Spirit of the One who raised Jesus from the dead dwells in you, the same one who raised Christ Jesus from the dead, he will also give life to your mortal bodies through

[460] Daniel R. Huber. Editorial. (Costa Rica, C. A. Publicadora la Merced. 2021. Artículo publicado en la Revista La Antorcha de la Verdad. Marzo-abril, 2021. Volumen 35. Número 2.), 3.

[461] I Peter 1:18-21, (KJV, 1960).

[462] Hebrews 13:20

[463] Acts 2:24, (NIV).

His Spirit dwells in you".[464] The apostle Peter said, "For Christ Himself suffered death for our sins, once and for all. He was innocent, but he suffered for the wicked, to bring you to God. In his human frailty, he died; but he was resurrected with a spiritual life".[465]

3. *That it was the same power of Jesus that resurrected his body.* The apostle Paul said, "What I want is to know Christ, to feel in me ***the power of his resurrection*** and solidarity in his sufferings; making myself like him in his death, I hope to come to the resurrection of the dead".[466] In the Gospel of John, Jesus said to the Jews, "Destroy this temple, and in three days I will raise it again". Later in his earthly ministry he said, "The Father loves me because I give my life to receive it again. No one takes my life, but I give it of my own free will. I have the right to give it and to receive it again".[467]

Wow!!! this is amazing! Someone has said that there is no worse blind man than the one who does not want to see. There is sufficient biblical and historical evidence to ensure the Resurrection of Jesus. They are proofs that God left as a testimony because the Resurrection of Jesus is an essential event for Christianity.

I understand that "some are troubled when they hear that the Father is God, that the Son is God, and that the Holy Spirit is God, and yet there are not three gods in the Trinity, but only one God; and they try to understand how this can be; especially when it is said that the Trinity acts inseparably in all of God's operations; yet it was not the voice of the Son,

---

[464]   Romans 8:11, (NBLA).

[465]   I Peter 3:18, (DHH).

[466]   Philippians 3:10-11, (DHH). The **Bolds** and the *Italics* are mine.

[467]   John 2:23-24; 10:17-18, (DHH).

but that of the Father, that resonated; only the Son appeared in mortal flesh, suffered, rose again, and ascended to heaven; and only the Holy Spirit came in the form of a dove".[468]

II.- THE SPIRIT WHO RESURRECTED JESUS WILL RESURRECT US.

The news of the newspaper La Opinión, on Thursday, August 19 (2021), announced that: "Haiti is living bleak days. After an earthquake struck the Caribbean Island on Saturday (Aug. 14) — leaving at least 2,100 people dead — another natural disaster came to hit its inhabitants once again: Tropical Storm Grace. Heavy rains and strong winds have made difficult the complex rescue work among the debris left by the earthquake of magnitude 7.2".[469] Nothing nice! Pain, sadness, despair, anguish and hopelessness.

However, when we think and believe that Jesus Christ overcame the grave and death itself, we find hope amid the catastrophe. The Bible assures us that the Spirit who raised Jesus will raise us up in His holy will and at His time.

One of the great Pauline statements that assures an afterlife says: "And if the Spirit of the one who raised Jesus lives in you, the same one who raised Christ will give new life to your mortal bodies through the Spirit of God who lives in you".[470] It is very true that when this body dies, because it is mortal, it

---

[468] Augustine of Hippo. *The Trinity*. (San Bernardino, California. Ivory Falls Books.2017), 8

[469] BBC News World. *Earthquake in Haiti*: "We are abandoned, and people are desperate for food, for some help." (La Habra, California. Internet. Article published on August 19, 2021. Retrieved August 20, 2021), ¿? https://laopinion.com/2021/08/19/terremoto-en-haiti-estamos-abandonados-y-la-gente-esta-desesperada-por-comida-por-algo-de-ayuda/?utm_source=La%20Opini%C3%B3n%20

[470] Romans 8:11, (DHH).

will return to the dust from which it was made, but, that is not the end of the individual, in some miraculous way, wherever his body has been, from there, the power of the same Spirit who raised Jesus, will also resurrect them; somehow miraculously, God will bring the atoms and all the components of the human being together again and give them life again.

The reading from Romans 8:9-11 clearly teaches that: "God assures in a clear and unmistakable way that his Spirit has established his dwelling place in the hearts of – all Christians – so, even if their bodies die, He will raise them from the dead, just as He did with Jesus".[471] All of us who have sincerely made a commitment to Jesus Christ to love Him, to serve Him, and to make Him our only God, we will be resurrected!

Now, this is essential in the Christian life; that is, without the Resurrection of Jesus in Christianity there is no hope that human beings who have given their lives to Jesus Christ will be resurrected to a better and eternal eschatological life. If we take away the essential value of the biblical accounts of his divine inspiration, we run the risk of making the Resurrection of Jesus a myth; something non-essential. The Bible and all its accounts are of vital essence to Christianity because they all give satisfactory hope and of course essential security. Hence, the Resurrection of Jesus, as narrated in the writings of the New Testament, are essential to Christian Doctrine.

When a select group of Catholic priests are considering that: "The Bible is no longer a literal text",[472] they are putting their finger on the flame of divinity and are in danger of burning

---

[471]   John Piper. *The Spirit will give life to your mortal bodies.* (City of Commerce, California. Fuerza Latina Entertainment Inc. April 2014), 4.

[472]   Hector G. Barnés. *IAN CALDWELL PUBLISHES 'THE FIFTH GOSPEL' (What I Discovered After Spending 11 Years Researching the Vatican).* (La Habra, California. Internet. Article published on May 3, 2015. Retrieved September 20, 2021), ¿? https://www.elconfidencial.com/alma-corazon-vida/2015-03-05/lo-que-descubri-despues-de-pasar-11-anos-investigando-al-vaticano_721525/

themselves and making others burn. Dustin Thompson, researching Vatican affairs, "stumbled upon one of the findings he considers most surprising after interviewing the first priest"[473] that had helped him in writing one of his books. "He explained to him the process of Bible study followed by seminarians; specifically, what is known as the synoptic gospels, three of the four canonical gospels (those of Matthew, Mark, and Luke), which coincide in most of their descriptions of the life of Jesus".[474] In this process of study, what they are doing is discrediting the Bible. And since the Bible mentions the Resurrection of Jesus and, this event is something essential for Christianity, then, we return to what the Apostle Paul said: "For if the dead are not resurrected, then neither is Christ resurrected; and if Christ is not resurrected, the message we preach is worthless, so is the faith you have, they are not worth anything".[475]

Was the Resurrection of Jesus Christ discredited by the apostle Paul? In no way! He told the brothers of the city of Corinth the following: "... I have taught them the same tradition that I received, namely, that Christ died for our sins, according to the Scriptures; that he was buried and that he was resurrected on the third day, also according to the Scriptures; and that he appeared to Cephas, and then to the twelve. He then appeared to more than five hundred of his followers at once, most of whom are still alive, although some have already died. Then he appeared to James, and then to all the apostles. Finally, He appeared to me as well..."[476]

---

[473] Hector G. Barnés. *IAN CALDWELL PUBLISHES 'THE FIFTH GOSPEL' (What I Discovered After Spending 11 Years Researching the Vatican).* (La Habra, California. Internet. Article published on May 3, 2015.

[474] Hector G. Barnés. *IAN CALDWELL PUBLISHES 'THE FIFTH GOSPEL' (What I Discovered After Spending 11 Years Researching the Vatican).* (La Habra, California. Internet. Article published on May 3, 2015. Retrieved September 20, 2021), ¿? https://www.elconfidencial.com/alma-corazon-vida/2015-03-05/lo-que-descubri-despues-de-pasar-11-anos-investigando-al-vaticano_721525/

[475] I Corinthians 15:13-14, (DHH).

[476] I Corinthians 15:3-8, (DHH).

Paul had no doubt that Jesus had risen. For Paul, the Resurrection of Jesus was essential in his life. And now, the Resurrection of Jesus is something essential to Christianity!

And yet, not only is it the purpose of discrediting the Bible, but the group of seminarians, according to the researcher, "emphasized them to forget about the accessory and focus on the essentials: 'Priests are being trained to put scripture under the microscope. To allow, and even insist, that there are parts of the gospels that should not be interpreted as history'."[477] And, if the Resurrection of Jesus is not part of the biblical account, then it ceases to be essential to Christianity.

So, if the Resurrection of Jesus is not essential to Christianity, then all preaching that refers to Jesus Christ is vain, hollow, without historical foundation. If this is so, there is no reason to celebrate the events of The Last Week of Jesus' earthly life.

Let's go back to Biblical Hermeneutics. *If there are some parts of the gospels that should not be interpreted as History*, or of some other biblical account, then the Bible has historical errors and if it does, then it is not the Word of God, for the Lord is not wrong, otherwise he is not God. And, if it is not God, then Jesus will not raise us up on the *eschaton*![478] Our assurance in the Risen Christ is vain!

---

[477]   Hector G. Barnés. *IAN CALDWELL PUBLISHES 'THE FIFTH GOSPEL' (What I Discovered After Spending 11 Years Researching the Vatican).* (La Habra, California. Internet. Article published on May 3, 2015. Retrieved September 20, 2021), ¿? https://www.elconfidencial.com/alma-corazon-vida/2015-03-05/lo-que-descubri-despues-de-pasar-11-anos-investigando-al-vaticano_721525/

[478]   Mario Alberto Molina. *Eschaton.* "Eschaton" is a Greek word. In the Christian vocabulary it designates those definitive realities that transcend human history: the resurrection of the dead, divine judgment, heaven and eternal happiness with God or damnation and hell. (La Habra, California. Internet. Article published on July 21, 2018, at 0:07h. Retrieved September 20, 2021), ¿? https://www.prensalibre.com/opinion/el-escaton/ eterna con Dios o la condenación y el infierno. (La Habra, California. Internet. Artículo publicado el 21 de julio de 2018 a las 0:07h. Consultado el 20 de septiembre del 2021), ¿? https://www.prensalibre.com/opinion/el-escaton/

Don't be fooled. Although an elite of wise men question the inspiration of the Bible, it remains the Word of God and the Resurrection of Jesus essential to Christianity. Yes, Jesus Christ will resurrect us up in the last days!

III.- THE ESSENCE OF THE RESURRECTION OF JESUS: LIFE!

As Jesus ministered bodily on this earth, one day he said to his disciples, "I am the way, the truth, and *the life*. Only by me can the Father be reached".[479] Science has striven to find the origin of life. And, when "*Life*," that is, Jesus Christ, manifested Itself to human beings, they did not receive it. The apostle John said that "*Life*"," to his own came, but they did not receive it.[480] *First,* this text speaks of the land of Israel and the Jews, they did not accept him as the Messiah of God. *Second,* by extension, many others from different nations have not accepted it either. The essence of Jesus' Resurrection is still being rejected. Life in Christ Jesus seems to remain a dilemma that is against science

Why this fear of being a Christian? Why this doubt about the effectiveness of Jesus' resurrection? Why doubt that by uniting human life to the life of the Risen One there is an eternal guarantee? "Many people try not to unite their lives to Christ by asserting that if something cannot be scientifically proven, it means that it is something false, or something that cannot be accepted. Contemporary man considers him too intelligent for him to accept Christ as the Redeemer or believe in the Resurrection"[481] of Jesus of Nazareth.

---

[479]   John 14:6, (DHH). **Bold** and I*talics* are mine.
[480]   John 1:11.
[481]   Josh McDowell. *What is this teaching?* (The Spirit will give life to your mortal bodies. (City of Commerce, California. Fuerza Latina Entertainment Inc. April 2014), 14.

In a very simple way that is still a scientific reality that the Bible supports one hundred percent is this statement: "... Science states that we need at least four elements to survive: 1.- *Water*. 2.-*Air*. 3.- *Food* and 4.- *Light*. When we read the Bible, we notice what JESUS said about himself. He who had ministered on this earth and who was crucified, killed, and now Risen Said:

1. *I am the Source of Living Water.* This is the idea of eternity. This means that Jesus is eternal. His resurrection confirms this biblical and theological truth. In Isaiah's prophecy concerning the Servant of God; the Promised Messiah is called," *"Eternal Father."* The prophet Micah prophesied about the reign of the deliverer from Bethlehem, and said, "But you, Bethlehem Ephratha, small to be among the families of Judah, will come out of you who will be Lord in Israel; and their departures are from the beginning, from the days of eternity". John's testimony is that: "In the beginning was the Word, and the Word was with God, and the Word was God. This was in the beginning with God".[482]

2. *I Am Breath of Life.* When Jesus Christ resurrected Lazarus of Bethany, He made two important statements. The first was: "I am the resurrection and the life; he who believes in me, even if he dies, will live. The second was: and everyone who lives and believes in me will never die".[483]

3. *I am the Bread of Life.* In Jesus' discourse delivered on the mountain on the shore of Lake Tiberias, he said

---

[482]   Isaiah 9:6; Micah 5:2; John 1:1-2, (KJV, 1960).
[483]   John 11:25–26, (LBLA).

to his hungry listeners, "I am the bread that gives life. He who comes to me will never be hungry; and he who believes in me will never thirst".[484]

4. *I am the Light of the World.* In the prologue of John's Gospel are these statements: "The Word gave life to all creation, and his life brought light to all. The light shines in the darkness, and the darkness can never extinguish it". Immediately afterwards, John, speaking of Jesus Christ Himself, said, "He who is the true light, who gives light to all, came into the world".[485]

Hallelujah! science got it right: We need JESUS to live!"[486] That same Spirit who raised Jesus from the dead is the same one who, in Christ Jesus, NOT only guarantees survival, but even more, guarantees Eternal Life. And this is essential for Christianity!

So essential is the Resurrection of Christ to Christianity that it is an event regarded "as one of the seven major events in the history of the universe, from the beginning of history to the end. The chronological order of these events is: (1) The creation of the angelic hosts (Col. 1:16); (2) the creation of the material universe and man (Gen. 1:1-31); (3) the incarnation (Jn. 1:14); (4) the death of Christ (Jn 19:30); (5) the resurrection of Christ (Matt. 28:5, 6); (6) the Second Coming of Christ (Rev. 19:1-16); and (7) the creation of the new heavens and the new earth (Rev. 21:1; Isa. 65:17)."[487]

---

[484]   John 6:35, (DHH).

[485]   John 1:4-5, 9, (NLT).

[486]   *Add on the Facebook of Joaquín Pérez Negrete.* La Habra, California. Internet. Statement published on 17 September 2017. Retrieved August 19, 2021.

[487]   Lewis Sperry Chafer. Systematic theology; Tomo I. Trds. Evis Carballosa, Rodolfo Mendieta P. and M. Francisco Lievano P. (Dalton, Georgia E. U. A. Publicaciones Españolas. 1974), 354. *Bolds* and *Italics* are mine.

In a poetic way, the apostle Paul rejoices in the Resurrection of Jesus and its consequences by saying: "Not all of us will die, but we will all be transformed in a moment, in the blink of an eye, when the last trumpet sounds. For the trumpet will sound, and the dead will be resurrected so as not to die again. And we will be transformed. For our corruptible nature will be clothed in the incorruptible, and our mortal body will be clothed in immortality. And when our corruptible nature has been clothed in the incorruptible, and when our mortal body has been clothed in immortality, the Scripture says this will be fulfilled: 'Death has been devoured by victory. Where is your victory, O death? Where is your sting, O death?'".[488] So: "Through Jesus Christ, we recognize the reality of the resurrection, and through his promise we appropriate it at the consummation".[489]

In the light of the Bible, there is no doubt that, first, there is the resurrection of the dead and, second, that Christ Jesus rose again. Thus, then, "the doctrine of the resurrection of the dead is the foundation of all Christianity".[490] Why? Because the essence of Jesus' resurrection: Is life!

CONCLUSION.

From the biblical point of view, Jesus was resurrected on the third day according to the Scriptures! The apostles Peter and John were eyewitnesses that the tomb was empty on the

---

[488] I Corinthians 15:51-53, (DHH).

[489] Simon J. Kistemaker. *Commentary on the New Testament: I Corinthians.* (Grand Rapids, Michigan. Challenge books. Published by Baker Book House. 1998), 638.

[490] Carroll, B. H. *Bible Commentary: James, Wrath and 2nd Thessalonians, 1st and 2nd Corinthians. Volume 10.* Trd. Sara A. Hale. (Terrassa (Barcelona), Spain. Editorial CLIE. 1987), 275.

morning of the third day after it had been buried.[491] That same day, Jesus presented himself to the rest of the disciples to confirm his resurrection.[492]

Without being opened the door of the place where the apostles were gathered, the Risen Jesus entered, showed himself to them and to assure them that it was him, "showed them the wounds of his hands and his side. They were overly filled with joy when they saw the Lord!"[493]

Many years later, when the apostle John wrote the book of Revelation, he initiated it at the request or command of the Risen Christ. John was imprisoned on the island of Patmos because he was preaching the Gospel of Jesus Christ and it was there, where the Risen Christ Jesus appears to him in a much more admirable glory than that occasion, he said: "And we saw his glory, glory like that of the only begotten of the Father, full of grace and truth".[494]

So sublime and admirable was that glorious presence that John said, "When I saw him, I fell at his feet as if dead".[495] And then he says some words that again prove that Jesus of Nazareth, the one who was crucified and buried on the edges of the city of Jerusalem, in Palestine, is not dead! It is Jesus Christ Risen! Notice what John says: "... But he put his right hand on me and said, 'Don't be afraid! I am the First and the Last. I am the one who lives. I was dead but look! Now I am alive forever and ever! And I have in my possession the keys of death and of the grave'."[496] Jesus Christ was resurrected! An essential fact for Christianity!

---

[491]   Luke 24:12: John 20:1-10.

[492]   John 20:19-22.

[493]   Matthew 20:20, (NLT).

[494]   John 1:14, (KJV, 1960.

[495]   Revelation 1:17th, (NIV).

[496]   Revelation 1:17b-18, (NIV).

TO FINISH THE READING OF THIS BOOK

Pastor Aaron Burgner has said that: "The Bible is a great story of one person, and that person is Jesus Christ. He is the hero of history whether in the Old Testament, or on the eschaton[497] or in creation, everything points to the Lord Jesus Christ in whom salvation is found".[498] In this book we have not touched on the whole history of Salvation, but only a part, he said, a small part of the history of *The Last Week* of the Great History of Salvation in Christ Jesus.

So, to end with this series of messages that I have titled: *The Last Week, first*; Let's think about what Santiago Wadel has written in his article: *God is... The good God,* in whom he has said that God is good, because He gives us His promises

---

[497] Mario Alberto Molina. *"Eschaton"* is a Greek word. In the Christian vocabulary it designates those definitive realities that transcend human history: the resurrection of the dead, divine judgment, heaven and eternal happiness with God or damnation and hell. (La Habra, California. Internet. Article published in the Prensa Libre on July 21, 2018 at 0:07h. Retrieved August 26, 2021), ¿? https://www.prensalibre.com/opinion/el-escaton/

[498] Aaron Burgner. *Comment on the page of the Indigenous Educational Center in Córdoba, Veracruz, Mexico.* (La Habra, California. Internet. Comment published by the CEI on July 27, 2020. Retrieved August 26, 2021), ¿? https://www.facebook.com/centroeducativoindigena/

and fulfills them. He says, "We have received many blessings from our good God, but there are many other blessings to come. How do we know? Because God has given us many promises, and the Bible qualifies them as 'precious', and 'great' (2 Peter 1:3-4)".[499]

They are promises that we find throughout the Bible, for example: "When the Israelites had already conquered the promised land, Joshua testified",[500] saying: "Not a single one of all the good promises that the Lord had made to the family of Israel was left unfulfilled; everything he had said came true".[501] Years later, the apostle Paul told the brethren of the Corinthian Church "that 'all the promises of God are in him Yes, and in him Amen'. This means that everything God promises is true (Yes) and certain (Amen)".[502]

Secondly: There was a divine agreement. From eternity, the Holy Trinity had promised the salvific plan. And since God is the God who fulfills His promises, He did it through the sacrifice of Christ Jesus! The Lord Jesus Christ became the Passover Lamb who, in that Last Week of earthly life, gave his life to fulfill all that was promised from eternity. The apostle Paul expresses this truth in these words: "But God, who is rich in mercy, by his great love with which he loved us, even though we were dead in sins, gave us life together with Christ (by grace you are saved), and together with him he raised us up, and also made us sit in the heavenly places with

---

[499] Santiago Wadel. *God is... Some attributes of God. The good God.* (Costa Rica, C. A. Publicadora la Merced. 2021. Article published in the magazine La Antorcha de la Verdad. March-April, 2021. Volume 35. Number 2.), 7.

[500] Santiago Wadel. *God is... Some attributes of God. The good God.* (Costa Rica, C. A. Publicadora la Merced. 2021. Article published in the magazine La Antorcha de la Verdad. March-April, 2021. Volume 35. Number 2.), 7.

[501] Josué 21:45, (NTV).

[502] Santiago Wadel. *God is... Some attributes of God. The good God.* (Costa Rica, C. A. Publicadora la Merced. 2021. Article published in the magazine La Antorcha de la Verdad. March-April, 2021. Volume 35. Number 2.), 7.

Christ Jesus, to show in the centuries to come the abundant riches of his grace in his goodness to us in Christ Jesus".[503]

God fulfilled in Christ Jesus His promise of salvation. Christ fulfilled all prophesied Scripture without leaving any of it to expectation. At the farewell, the night before He was arrested, Jesus prayed for His disciples and promised them that He would send them to the Comforter; that is, the Holy Spirit, so that he would be with them all the time and thus, they could have courage and protection from God. Before ascending to His Father's side, Jesus promised His followers that He would be with them *always*.[504] Let us remember that *"his promises in him are Yes and in himself, they are Amen."* That is, they are true and safe.

The very fact that he rose from the dead guarantees that what he did and said in *The Last Week* of his life on this earth is a strong salvific foundation and faith that, in addition to Jesus Christ being faithful in keeping his word, it also assures us of an eternity of glory at his side.

Eleazar Barajas
La Habra, California.
January 2022

---

[503]   Ephesians 2:4-7, (KJV, 1960).
[504]   John 15-16; Matthew 28:16-20.

Bibliography

The Last Week

Ang, Gonzalo (director). Reader's Digest. *Jesus and His Time. The Easter pilgrimages.* (Mexico. Rider's Digest Mexico S.A. de C.V. 2000).

Aquinas, St. Thomas of. Cantena Aurea: *Evangelical Commentaries: St. Luke.* (San Bernardino, California. USED. Ivory Falls Books. 2006).

Aquinas, St. Thomas of. Cantena Aurea: *Commentaries on the Gospel of John.* (San Bernardino, California. USED. Ivory Falls Books. 2019).

Barclay, William. *Commentary on the New Testament: Volume 2*: MATTHEW: II. Trd. Alberto Araujo. (Terrassa (Barcelona), Spain. Editorial CLIE. 1997).

Barclay, William. *Commentary on the New Testament: Volume 4: LUKE.* (Terrassa (Barcelona), Spain. Editorial CLIE. 1994).

Barclay, William. *Commentary on the New Testament: Volume 6: JOHN: II.* (Terrassa (Barcelona), Spain. Editorial CLIE. 1996).

Barclay, William. *Commentary on the New Testament: Volume 9: CORINTHIANS.* (Terrassa (Barcelona), Spain. Editorial CLIE. 1996).

Barclay William. *Commentary on the New Testament: Volume 10: Galatians and Ephesians.* (Terrassa (Barcelona), Spain. Editorial CLIE. 1970).

Barclay, William. *Commentary on the New Testament: Volume 12: Wrath and 2 Timothy, Titus, and Philemon.* (Terrassa (Barcelona), Spain. Editorial CLIE. 1998).

Barclay, William. *Commentary on the New Testament: Volume 15: 1st, 2nd, 3rd of John and Jude.* Td. Alberto Araujo. (Terrassa (Barcelona), Spain. Editorial CLIE. 1998).

Bermudes, Kittim Silva. *Daniel: History and Prophecy.* (Viladecavalls, (Barcelona), Spain. Editorial CLIE. 2014).

NVI Archaeological Study Bible: An Illustrated Journey to Raves of Biblical Culture and History. (Miami, Florida. Editorial Vida. 2009).

Schematic Study Bible. (Brazil. United Bible Societies. 2010).

Peshito Bible in Spanish. (Nashville, Tennessee. Published by Holman Bible Publishers. 2000), 1076.

Bock, L. Darrell. *Bible Commentary with Application: LUCAS. From the biblical text to a contemporary application.* (Miami, Florida. Editorial Vida. 2011).

Blanchard, Ken and Phil Hodges. *A leader like Jesus.* (Nashville, Tennessee, USA. Nelson Group. 2012).

Bramsen, P.S. *One God a message: Discover the mystery: Make the old man.* (Grand Rapids, Michigan. Editorial Portavoz, a subsidiary of Kregel Publications. 2011).

Calcada, S. Leticia. General Edition. *Holman Illustrated Bible Dictionary.* (Nashville, Tennessee. B&H Publishing Group. 2008).

Carro, Daniel, José Tomás Poe and Rubén O. Zorzoli (General Editors). *Hispanic World Bible Commentary: Volume 8: PSALMS.* (El Paso, Texas. Editorial Mundo Hispano.2002).

Carroll, B. H. *Bible Commentary: The Four Gospels. Volume 6. Volume II.* Trd. Sara A. Hale. (Terrassa (Barcelona), Spain. Editorial CLIE. 1986).

Carroll, B. H. *Bible Commentary: James, Wrath and 2nd Thessalonians, 1st and 2nd Corinthians. Volume 10.* Trd. Sara A. Hale. (Terrassa (Barcelona), Spain. Editorial CLIE. 1987).

Chafer, Sperry Lewis. *Systematic theology; Tomo I.* Trds. Evis Carballosa, Rodolfo Mendieta P. and M. Francisco Lievano P. (Dalton, Georgia E. U. A. Publicaciones Españolas. 1974).

Edersheim. Alfred. *The Temple: His ministry and services in the time of Christ.* (Terrassa (Barcelona), Spain. Editorial CLIE. 1990).

F. F. Bruce. *The Epistle to the Hebrews.* (Grand Rapids, Michigan. New Creation and William B. Eerdmans Publishing Company. 1987).

Glaser, Mitch. Isaiah 53: *An explanation. This chapter will change your life.* (New York, USA. Chosen People Productions. 2010).

Guthrie, H, George. *Comment with application: HEBREWS. From the biblical text to a contemporary application.* (Miami, Florida. Editorial Vida. 2014).

Hendriksen, William. *The Gospel of Matthew: Commentary on the New Testament.* (Grand Rapids, Michigan. Distributed by T.E.L.L. Subcommittee On Christian Literature. 1986).

Henry Matthew. *Exegetical-Devotional Commentary on the Entire Bible: Matthew.* Td. Francisco Lacueva. (Terrassa (Barcelona), Spain. Editorial CLIE. 1984).

Hippo, Augustine of. *The Trinity.* (San Bernardino, California. Ivory Falls Books.2017).

Holy Bible. Red Letter Edition. (Chicago, Illinois. The John A. Hertel CO. 1960).

Kenyon, W. E. *In His Presence: A Revelation of Who We Are in Christ.* Trds Belmonte Translators. (New Kensington, PA. Whitaker House. 2014).

Kistemaker J. Simon. *Commentary on the New Testament: I Corinthians.* (Grand Rapids, Michigan. Challenge Books. Published by Baker Book House. 1998).

The Bible of the Americas: Study Bible. (Nashville, Tennessee. Edited by The Lockman Foundation. Published by B&H Publishing Group. 2000).

Latina, strength. *Revista Cristiana en Español.* (City of Commerce, California. Fuerza Latina Entertainment Inc. April 2014).

Lucan, Max. *For these difficult times: Look to heaven for hope and healing.* (Nashville, Tennessee, USA. Nelson Group. 2006).

Lee, Witness. *The heavenly ministry of Christ.* (Anaheim, California. Living Stream Ministry www.ism.org. 2003).

Macarthur, John. *A Perfect Life: The Complete Story of the Lord Jesus.* (Nashville, Tennessee. Nelson Group Inc. A registered trademark of Thomas Nelson Inc. 2012).

Moo, J. Douglas. *Romans: Commentary with application; from the biblical text to a contemporary application.* (Miami, Florida. Editorial Vida. 2011).

Nelson, Eduardo G., Mervin Breneman, Ricardo Souto Copeiro and others. *Hispanic World Bible Commentary: Psalms: Volume 8.* (El Paso, Texas. Editorial Mundo Hispano. 2002).

Perez, Millos Samuel. *Exegetical commentary on the Greek text of the New Testament: JOHN.* (Viladecavalls (Barcelona), Spain. Editorial CLIE. 2016).

Perez, Millos Samuel. *Exegetical commentary on the Greek text of the New Testament: Ephesians.* (Viladecavalls (Barcelona), Spain. Editorial CLIE. 2010).

Perez, Millos Samuel. *Exegetical commentary on the Greek text of the New Testament: HEBREWS.* (Viladecavalls (Barcelona), Spain. Editorial CLIE. 2009).

Reader's Digest Selections Magazine. (New York. USED. Reader's Digest Inc. Selections Section: Achievers. August 2006).

Stanley, Charles F. Bible Principles of Life. (Nashville, Tennessee, USA. Nelson Group. 2010).

Strobel, Lee. *The Case of Christ: A Thorough Investigation.* Trd. Lorena Loguzzo. (Miami, Florida. Editorial Vida. 2000).

New World Translation of the Holy Scriptures. (New, York. USED. Watch Tower Bible and Tract Society of Pennsylvania e International Bible Students Association of Brooklyn, New York. 1961).

Vila, Samuel. *Explanatory Encyclopedia of Biblical Difficulties.* (Terrassa, (Barcelona), Spain. CLIE Books. 1990).

Wadel Santiago. *God is... Some attributes of God. The good God.* (Costa Rica, C. A. Publicadora la Merced. 2021.

Article published in the magazine La Antorcha de la Verdad. March-April 2021. Volume 35. Number 2.).

Wilkins, Michael J. *Bible Commentary with Application: MATTHEW: From the Biblical Text to a Contemporary Application.* (Nashville, Tennessee, USA. Editorial Vida. 2016).

Eleazar Barajas
January 2022
La Habra, California

Printed in the United States
by Baker & Taylor Publisher Services